WHAT THEY SAY
IN NEW ENGLAND

A BOOK OF SIGNS, SAY-
INGS, AND SUPERSTITIONS

COLLECTED

BY

CLIFTON JOHNSON

AUTHOR OF " THE NEW ENGLAND COUNTRY
" THE FARMER'S BOY " ETC.

BOSTON
LEE AND SHEPARD PUBLISHERS
10 MILK STREET
1896

WHAT THEY SAY IN NEW ENGLAND

C. J. Peters & Son, Typographers,
Presswork by Rockwell and Churchill, Boston, U S A

CONTENTS

OF

WHAT THEY SAY
IN NEW ENGLAND

· ·

6   Contents

INTRODUCTORY

· ·

WHEN I began to collect these signs and sayings, it was with the idea of gathering them for my own entertainment. In days like the present of universal books and schools, I thought I could hope to get only a few remnants of the thought and notions that have descended to us from the illiterate and superstitious ages of the past; and I supposed that by the time I had picked up two or three scores of these oddities the subject would be exhausted as far as New England was concerned. But when I began to notice, I found that people in their every-day conversation were constantly dropping remarks on the significance of all sorts of things that were a part of this old folk-lore. When questioned, nearly every one, old and young, could repeat a few sayings of the kind I sought, and among these were almost always some I had not heard before. My collection

7

grew until I saw the possibility of a
volume, and I could not but wonder
what the superstitions of the Dark Ages
were like if these were only remnants.
Not only was the number of sayings
floating about astonishing, but it was
remarkable how much belief there was
in them

Most New Englanders disclaim a belief in signs, — at least, they say a good
share of them are all nonsense: yet a
confidential acquaintance is apt to re-
veal some they accept Most of the
signs you hear from any particular person are repeated because they are simply curious, or because there may be
some possible unperceived significance
in them I do not suppose any one
believes them all, unless it is some imaginative small boy. It is the least
thoughtful and least educated classes
that have most belief in signs. Children accept them readily, just as they
will accept anything told them about
which they know nothing to the contrary.
Some sayings add charm, some mystery,
to the child's life, others frighten The
person who is not affected at all by
these old sayings is the exception. A
few of them, as, for instance, certain of

those about the weather, have a scien-
tific foundation; and I do not speak of
those, but of such as seem to be entirely without sense It is not always
easy to decide which sayings have truth
to back them and which only fancy. If
you will listen to the relation of them,
some of the most fantastic will be told
with such detail and so stoutly cham-
pioned that you are tempted to question
if the days of miracles really are past.
A man will tell you about horse-hairs
turning into snakes; and you will hear of
wart cures, and of the good or ill effect
of one thing and another, — and all of
the list "known" to be true, — till you
begin to think that perhaps your own
knowledge of the supernatural is very
narrow and bigoted.

Perhaps no class is more addicted to
sign-telling and belief in signs than
those who have emigrated to this country in comparatively recent years. It is
their children at the schools who are
most apt to keep the rest posted as to
what means what, and as to when things
portend disaster.

I do not know that any of the signs
gathered are natives of New England
by right of invention. I suppose most

can be traced to a foreign ancestry, just
as they say all the old jokes can be
traced back to Noah. Yet if Yankee
cuteness did not share in the originating
of them, it has given its peculiar local
twist to a large number of them.

One man who has made a study of
the subject affirms that superstition, in
our most cultured communities, is so
general that no woman in Massachusetts, for instance, would invite a party
of thirteen to dine together. There are
plenty of women who would not themselves object to being one of a dinner
party of thirteen; but they would not
call together such a number, because
among the guests there would be sure
to be some who would be disturbed.
The statement seems to me too sweeping, though I think there is much truth
in it; and I have known parties which
happened to number thirteen where
great pains were taken to procure an
extra guest, or to have a part of those
present eat at a side-table. It is certain that signs and sayings flourish in the
society life of our towns. Indeed, you
cannot tell with certainty who will believe them and who disbelieve; for there
are still men of wise repute and high

position who have superstitions that lead
them to performances as odd as that of
Dr. Johnson, who would always touch
every post in a certain street when he
passed through

There are many believers in the significance of dreams, and they can give
plenty of instances in their own expe-
rience and that of others to show a good
foundation for their faith. I suppose
this faith and apparent proof grow out
of the fact that we remember odd co-
incidences, and forget the many times
when we dreamed and nothing came
of it.

The moon gets seriously given credit
for a good many things too Yet how
its phases could affect the weather, or
the crops, or the pork of the hogs that
are killed, I do not understand, and
probably no one does I have read
that the light of the moon will spoil fish
exposed to it; but I am sure I do not
see what there could be in moonlight to
harm the fish or anything else.

Wart cures have a good many cham-
pions who have proved their virtues in
their own persons, most people who try
these cures believe in the last one they
tried before the warts left them It

doesn't matter how ridiculous it was, if the warts went, that settles it. Even Lord Bacon, that "wisest of men," tells us at length of a queer performance he once went through to dispose of his warts, and though he did what he did as an unbeliever, when the warts disappeared he was constrained to credit the value and efficacy of this method of wart cure.

Luck and snakes and charms, and all the rest of the list, have believers as well as quoters. Least weight is perhaps attached to the sentimental sayings and to fortune-telling Love signs are repeated and futures forecast usually for the humor of the thing, though I imagine there are persons who find even these oracular. Small children are much concerned over the way their buttons or the daisy petals count up; but as their fortune is different with different daisies or a change of clothes, they soon get over this There is rarely any one in country regions who makes pretensions to fortune-telling, though wandering gypsies, when they pass through a district, are ready for a consideration to tell what one's life will be. I think few people believe in the powers these gypsies claim, but some say they tell things they themselves had no idea were so, or would be so, until afterward.

One might fancy, from the number of sayings and superstitions that can be readily picked up, that there was as yet no real folk-lore decadence. But you will find when you talk with people that they are very sure to speak of a father or a grandfather or grandmother, or some other relative, now passed away, whom you "ought to have seen — they had no end of signs and they knew lots of old rhymes and songs, and believed in witches. They would be just the ones you're lookin' after." Signs are certainly not believed in as unquestioningly as they were once, nor are they in so common use. At the same time we lose them gradually, and the survivors will make up a large bulk in common use for a great while to come. Loss is most apparent when we get outside the short jingles and sayings of a sentence or two in length. There is now such a mass of reading, stories and songs, that people gather hastily and forget quickly. In more barren times many tales were handed down by word of mouth, and were remembered and repeated a life-

time through. As for songs, now we
have a new one that takes the popular
fancy every six months.   For half a
year everybody is singing it, and after
that nobody sings it.   In the olden time
the clever ones had a number of ditties
and ballads in their heads that were in-
delibly memorized, and at an evening
party, when they were called on for a
song, they could sing the particular song
they undertook clear through, even if
it had twenty-nine verses.   They could
tell old fairy-tales too, and would scare
themselves with witch stories.   Now, of
all this more elaborate lore, you can pick
up only scattered fragments.

Nearly all of what is in this volume
was gathered in western Massachusetts.
It is largely put down in the language
of the people who made the statements,
and I have sometimes added their comments.   With few exceptions, everything
in the book came to me by word of
mouth.

The chapter of Nursery Tales and
some other chapters could have been
much extended, but I did not care to
repeat things found in other books, unless there was an interesting individ-
uality in the telling that warranted it.

I would be glad if New England readers who know of sayings and stories not noted here would send such to me.

CLIFTON JOHNSON

HADLEY, MASS

Postscript. This book is one of three New England books that I have written, each of which in its way supplements the others. The titles of the two other books are "The New England Country," a study of old times and of the out-of-doors nature of the present, and "A Book of Country Clouds and Sunshine," a study of life on our farms and in our rural villages. Both books are very fully illustrated.

THE WEATHER

WHEN you see the sun drawing water at night, know that it will rain on the morrow. The sun is said to be drawing water when its rays can be seen shining through rifts in distant clouds.

> Rain before seven,
> Clear before 'leven.

As the old woman said, " I never knew it to begin in the mornin' and rain all day in my life. But I've known it to begin at noon and rain all day lots of times."

Six weeks after you hear the first katydid look for a frost.

Notice your cat when it washes its face. The paw it uses and the direction it faces will show the point of compass whence the wind is blowing. For instance, the cat faces the north and washes with its left paw; the wind is blowing from the north-west.

Blow out a candle, and if the wick

17

continues long to smoulder, look for bad weather. If it goes out quickly, the weather will be fair.

When the camphor in its bottle is "riley," it shows that a storm is brewing.

> Red in the morning,
> Sailors take warning;
> Red at night,
> Sailors delight.

There is a rainbow jingle much like this, which runs as follows : —

> Rainbow in the morning,
> Sailors take warning,
> Rainbow at night,
> Sailors delight,
> Rainbow at noon,
> Rain very soon.

When you hear the first frogs in the spring, you may know the frost is out of the ground

The last Friday of each month is the almanac index for the next month   If the weather is fair, the month will be likewise ; if foul, so will the month be

The twelve days after Christmas indicate the weather for the following year. Each day in order shows the weather for one month.

If it storms the first Sunday in the month, it will storm every Sunday in the month.

When you take up the tea-kettle and find sparks on the bottom, it is a sign of cold weather.

> Fog on the hills,
> More water for the mills.

When a person kills a snake he does well to consider what kind of weather he would like. If he hangs the snake up, it will rain ; if he buries it, the weather will be fair.

Rub a cat's back the wrong way, and if you see sparks, it is a sign of cold weather.

If the sun sets in a cloud, it will rain on the morrow. The person who takes this saying as literally true would do well to remember that unless the cloud that hides the sun from his sight is extremely large, a spectator a short distance to the north or south would at the same moment see the sun set in clear sky.

If you see sun-dogs, expect rain soon.

In winter when you see the wild geese flying south, expect cold weather. They fly south because the ponds to the

north are frozen over.   When the geese
are seen flying north, warm weather is
to be expected.

Three white frosts and then a storm.

When you see whitecaps on the pond
or river, it is going to rain

When the smoke from a chimney does
not rise, but falls to the ground, it is
going to storm

When the squirrels lay in a big store
of nuts, look for a hard winter.

Three foggy mornings and then a
rain

Between twelve and two
You can tell what the day will do.

An evening red and a morning gray
Will set the traveller on his way.
But an evening gray and a morning red
Will pour down rain on the traveller's
    head.

If the corn-husks are thicker than
usual, the winter will be colder than
usual.

If the melt of the hog killed in the
fall is big at the front end, the winter
will be sharpest at the beginning. If
the melt is biggest at the rear, the winter will be coldest in the latter part

If in the autumn you find the skin of

the apples tougher than usual, look for
a cold winter.

When the cattle lie down as soon as
they are turned out to pasture in the
morning, it is because they feel a rheumatic weariness in their bones, and you
can look for a rain soon

If the chickens' feathers are very
thick at Thanksgiving time, the winter
will be a hard one

A sunshiny shower
Won't last half an hour

A ringing in the ears is the sign of
a change of weather. Others say it is
a sign that several people are talking
about you.

When the rooster crows at nine
o'clock in the evening, expect a change
of weather

If the chickens come out while it rains,
it is a sign that the storm is to be a
long one If they stand around under
the shed, the storm will be short

If it rains on the first dog-day it will
rain on each of the other thirty-nine
If, on the other hand, the first dog-day
is dry, all the rest will be dry

If the chickweed blossoms are open,
it will not rain for at least three hours

When the fog goes up the mountain
    hoppin',
Then the rain comes down the moun-
    tain droppin'.

But if instead of rising the fog de-
scends, it is going to clear off.

If you see froth along the shores of
the streams, you may know it is going
to rain.

On such mornings as you see the cob-
webs on lawns and grass-fields shining
with dew, the day will be fair.

All signs fail in a dry time.

When the farm animals are unusually
frisky, it is a sign that it is going to rain.

If the breast-bones of the Thanksgiving chickens are light in color, there
will be a good deal of snow in the winter following   If the color is dark, there
will be little snow

When a night passes and no dew falls,
it is a sign it is going to rain.   This
omen loses much of its mystery when
one remembers that dew has not fallen
because the night was clouded.

Northern lights are a sign of cold
weather.

After the frogs begin to sing in the
spring, if they are frozen in three times,

you may be sure that afterwards you will have warm weather.

When the fire snaps and sparkles, it is a sign cold weather is coming.

If some night you hear a cricket chirping in the house, look for cold weather soon.

When the wind whistles about the house, that is a sign of a storm.

When you hear an owl hoot, it is safe to conclude it is going to storm

When you hear a cuckoo calling, you may know it is going to rain. Bob White sings at such times too. Some say he is calling, "More wet, more wet." When you hear the tree-toads crying, you can also know it is going to rain.

If the rooster crows on the fence, it is a sign that the weather is going to change.

If the rooster crows when he goes to
    bed,
He will get up with a wet head.

If the water boils out of the kettle, it is a sign that it is going to storm.

If the snow on the roof melts off, the next storm will be rain. If it blows off, you can calculate on snow.

The day of the month on which the first snowstorm comes gives the number of storms you can expect in the following winter.

If the breast-bone of the Thanksgiving goose is dark, it shows that you will have more rain in the succeeding winter than snow.

A mackerel sky
Won't leave the ground dry.

Another jingle referring to much the same kind of a clouded sky is this —

Mackerel scales and mares' tails
Make lofty ships to carry low sails

If you see an old cat running and playing and feeling good, it is a sign the wind is going to blow

The sun shines every Saturday but one in the year On some Saturdays there may not be more than a few stray gleams, but with the single exception it will at least shine a little

If the sun sets clear on Friday, it will storm before Monday night

Whistle when you want the wind to blow

A cold, wet May,
A barn full of hay.

If the cat comes in and sits on the

hearth with its back to the north, it is a sign of cold weather.

If you see the cat or the dog eating grass, you may look for rain soon.

If the children find the dog eating grass when they do not wish it to rain, they will chase him away, with the idea to in that way gain fair weather.

When the scales are thick on the buds, the winter will be long and cold.

If it rains while the sun shines, it will rain on the day following.

When it rains thus, the saying is that " the devil is whipping his wife."

When in the evening you see the swallows flying high, the morrow will be fair. When the swallows fly low, it is a sign of rain.

When the leaves of the poplars or other trees turn up their under sides, look for rain. Know, too, that it is going to rain when you see the hens "greasing" themselves.

When of a morning you find tiny heaps of dirt thrown up by the ants during the night in the hard-packed earth of the paths and dooryard, you can calculate on a fair day.

When the coals in the old fireplace were ruddy, and the fire burned up

brightly, it was said cold weather was
approaching. When the fire sparkled
and snapped, they expected wind.

A curdly sky is the sign of a rain
within three days

If the ice on the trees melts and runs
off, the next storm will be rain   If it is
cracked off by the wind, the storm that
comes next will be snow.

If you see an unusual number of crows
flying about in the autumn, look for a
cold winter   This is accounted a very
sensible saying by some, on the ground
that many more of the birds will nat-
urally be hovering about on their way
south when a hard winter is approaching than when the season promises to
be mild.

If the sky looks brassy in the west at
sunset, it is a sign of high winds

> When the wind is in the east,
> Then the sap will run the least.
> When the wind is in the west,
> Then the sap will run the best

Thunder after midnight means that
the next day will be lowery

If the sun shines clear in the early
morning, and then the sky very soon
clouds up, it will rain before night

When you see the frogs jumping around in the meadows with greater activity than common, look for rain soon.

When you hear the frogs piping of an evening, you can calculate on a fair morrow

When the chimney swallows flock out in great numbers, and dart about high in the air, diving and whirling in great excitement, there is soon to be a thunder-storm or a high wind

Snowy winter, a plentiful harvest. The snow is supposed to protect the roots of grass, vines, and trees, so that they put forth more vigorous growths the summer following

If March comes in like a lion, it goes out like a lamb If it comes in like a lamb, it will go out like a lion.

Kill a beetle, and it will be sure to bring rain

Snow that comes in the old of the moon is apt to last. Snow that comes in the new of the moon is apt to melt quickly.

April showers
Bring May flowers.

When you see the pigs carry straws in their mouths, look for high winds.

A peck of March dust is worth a bag of gold. The idea is that when you have much dust blowing about there must be much wind; and winds at that season dry the mud, and prepare the earth so that all crops can get an early start.

> Open and shet
> Sign of wet.

That is, you can expect rain when the clouds open and shut.

> When the wind is in the east,
> 'Tis neither good for man nor beast.

> Sun at seven,
> Rain at 'leven.

This means that if early in a cloudy morning the sun comes out for a little, it will rain by noon.

The sunlight always dawns on the wall on Easter morning.

Whenever after it has been raining you can see through the clouds enough blue sky to make a pair of Dutchman's breeches, you may know it is going to clear off.

> As far as the sun shines in on Candle-
> mas Day.
> So far the snow blows in before May
> Day.

If Candlemas day be fair and bright,
Winter will take another flight ,
If chance to fall a shower of rain,
Winter will not come again.

If Candlemas Day be bright and clear,
Be sure you will have two winters that
    year

If Candlemas Day be fair and clear,
All old men wish their wives on the
    bier

This savage rhyme must have descended from very ancient times.   The
idea is, that when the old man found
the second of February clear, and remembered that this meant there was still
hard winter weather ahead, he wished
his wife dead because of the trouble it
would be to support her

    On Candlemas Day
    Half the wood and half the hay

The old farmer at this time takes a
critical survey of his woodpile and hay-
mow; and if there is not in them half
what there was at the beginning of
winter, he lays plans for their replen-
ishing before the opening of the new
season.

Others say, —

> Half the pork and half the hay
> On Christmas Day.

It is related that there was a time when the men would occupy a part of their leisure on Christmas Day in making a tour of the neighbors to see how their hay was holding out.

If the woodchuck comes out on Candlemas Day, and sees his shadow, he crawls back to his hole and dozes again. He knows there will still be sharp weather. If the day is cloudy and he sees no shadow, he knows the hardest part of winter is past, and begins to make preparations for warm-weather housekeeping.

It's a sign of rain when the flies bite.

As long as the dogstar reigns, there will be dry weather.

"I was sure 'twas goin' to rain when I started out this mornin', it looked so dark and dull. Then I see one o' these little whirlwinds, and it turned around from right to left like you wind your watch, and I knew we wouldn't have no rain that day anyhow." A whirlwind has to turn from left to right to mean rain.

On some days of autumn you may
see the grass full of stringy lines of cob-
webs that make a glistening path sun-
ward.   They are a sign of frost.

When it begins to snow, notice the
size of the flakes.   If they are very fine,
the storm will be a long one; if large,
the storm will soon be over.

When you see a cloud in the sky that
grows larger, it is going to storm.   When
you see a cloud grow smaller and melt
away, it is going to be fair

There is going to be a change of
weather when you hear the telegraph
poles buzz It is going to be either
colder or warmer.

It is a sign of a storm when you see
the sheep feeding more eagerly than
usual.

If a storm clears off in the night, you
can expect another storm soon.

The bones of rheumatic people ache
when a storm is brewing

"Well, boys," says the farmer, "you
want to hustle round this morning and
get that hay in. My bones have been
achin', and there's always a storm within
forty-eight hours after they begin to
ache."

TEA-GROUNDS

WHEN you find tea-grounds floating in your cup, know that you are going to have company. If the grounds are soft, it is a woman who is coming; if hard, a man. If the grounds are long, the person coming is tall; if short, the visitor will be short. When a girl or woman first sights the floating grounds in her cup, the comment is apt to be, "There, got a beau!" If the grounds are taken out and thrown under the table, the company will stay all night. If the grounds are left in the cup, the visitor will simply make a call.

After you drink the tea you can get still further enlightenment, if there are grounds in the bottom of the cup. Turn the cup around a few times Then put it bottom upwards on your saucer, and give it a few more turns. Now turn it over. If you see paths in the grounds, it is a sign that you are to go on a journey   If the paths are long, the journey will be long, and *vue versâ*.   Turn the cup up sideways, and if any tea runs out you will cry on your journey.   If the grounds anywhere form a ring with a dot in the middle, that is a wish, and you must think what you most want.   You may see hills, and people walking or working or on horseback.   All the things you see have a meaning.   But I believe you are at liberty to interpret them pretty much as you choose.   It is to be noted that many people can see naught but the tea-grounds, where others see all sorts of objects in them.

DREAMS

IF you dream of falling, and are awa-
kened by the fancied jar of landing, it is
a sign that you are going to be sick. If,
however, you awake while still in mid-
air, you may be assured you will continue
in good health.

Tell your dreams, and you will keep
on dreaming. To tell the dreams cul-
tivates a habit of remembering what is
dreamed, and that is probably the only
effect, though it may apparently seem to
make the teller have more dreams.

Dream of seeing fresh beef, and you
will soon hear of a friend who is sick.

If you dream of water, it is a sign of
sickness

If you dream of eating. it is a sign that
you are going to be sick.

One woman says, " Well, I always
know I'm goin' to be sick when I dream
I can't get the table set. When I dream

34

there's so many here I can't get my
work done, I always have a sick spell."

It used to be said that if a dream was
sufficiently vivid to make the dreamer
notice and remember it, there was some
occult significance in it that was worthy
of study.

Dreams are often thought to contain
information   Sometimes the information
is in a realistic, sometimes in a symbolic
form.   Frequently the dreams contain
prophetic warnings.   Many still believe
in dreams to a limited degree.   The following are examples of what are repeated
as dreams of proved significance   An
old lady tells the first : —

"It was after midnight, and I was
dreaming a dream about a terrible thunder-storm.   It grew worse and worse till
there was one clap so loud it seemed as
if the skies had broken to pieces.   Right
after it I woke up, and I heard a knock
on the outside door of the sitting-room   I
knew that instant what my dream meant
and who was there   It was Charlie !   I
went to the door and it was   There he
had been gone seven or eight years.
He'd been a sailor on the ocean, and
we hadn't heard a word from him, and
didn't know but he was dead, and that

dream came to show me he was alive and near."

A younger woman tells the second · —

" I dreamed one night I was going to get a scolding letter from Centerville ; and the next day I got a scolding letter from Centerville, and it was word for word just as I dreamed it. Wa'n't that curious ?

"Don't you believe in dreams? There's lots do. Our minister does I asked him one day.

" ' Don't you believe in dreams ? ' says I.

" ' Yes, I do,' says 'e Most everybody believes in some of 'em."

A third woman relates the following

' One night toward morning I dreamed I saw Cousin Jane way up on the top of a high mountain, and I was looking up at her from the valley, and wondering how she got up there She was so high up it seemed as though her head touched the sky, and she looked down and smiled on me just as pleasant as could be I hunted around for some way to get up to her, and I found some steps But when I got half way up, the steps came to an end, and I couldn't get any farther. The next thing I found myself in a river and in lots of trouble. The waters were muddy, and the wind blew, and the waves dashed over me. Then I woke up, and there was beginning to be light enough to see things around in the room, so I knew it was time to get up. All that morning I felt downhearted and depressed, and I couldn't think of any reason why. Then at noon there came a telegram that Cousin Jane had died just before sunrise that day."

Dream of the dead, and you will hear from the living. That means, from a near relative of the deceased.

To dream of a funeral is a sign of a wedding

To dream of a wedding is a sign of a funeral.

Dreams go by contraries, it is said, and these last two examples are to the point. Nevertheless, it will be noted that most dreams are interpreted in accord with their incidents, and not reversibly.

If you dream of snakes, it is a sign you have an enemy.

If in your dreams you kill the snake, you may know you will get the best of your enemy.

If you dream of a fire, it is a sign

you are going to quarrel. If you dream
you put out the fire, you are the one who
is to conquer in the quarrel.

"There! I think there's more in those
two than in all the other signs put together. When I dream of fire, I'm very
careful what I do, so's not to get into
any quarrel; and if I dream of snakes, I
look out for folks for fear I'll meet an
enemy."

> Saturday night dream,
> Sunday morning told,
> Sign 'twill come to pass
> Before it's a week old.

"You will have great trouble if you
dream of a white horse," said Uncle
Timothy. "I've always found that to
come true. There was one time in particular I remember. It was winter, and
I was at work a good many miles from
home in a logging-camp. One night I
had a terrible dream about a white horse
that got angry with me, and bit me. I
knew something would happen in consequence of that dream, and I was afraid
I was going to get killed. I wa'n't
good for much workin' that day, I felt
so gloomy about my dream; but I went
out with my axe same as usual. I

wa'n't noticing things as I ought to,
and when I was cutting a tree, it came
down and knocked me senseless.   The
rest of the fellows carried me to camp
I can't tell you how relieved I was when
I come to and found myself alive.   I
thought myself lucky to get off so easy
after such a dream."

There are those, however, who say
that to dream of a white horse is a sign
you are going to be rich.

When you sleep in a strange bed,
whatever you dream will come to pass.

" But then one can see that that can't
be, for one dreams horrid dreams and
queer things that never could come to
pass."

If you dream of lice, it is a sign that
sickness threatens some member of the
family.

Tell your dream before breakfast, and
it will come to pass.

To dream of eggs is a sign of trouble

It is a good sign to dream of clear
water, but to dream of muddy water is
a sign of trouble.

Dream a thing three nights in succession, and it will come to pass

What you dream Monday morning
before daylight will come true before

Saturday night. If what you dream is bad, you can keep it from coming true by not telling your dream till after you've eaten breakfast.

To dream of picking blackberries is a sign of sickness

Sleep with a piece of wedding-cake under your pillow for three nights in succession, and whatever you dream of on the third night will come to pass.

"You can't always dream, though. I know I tried it when Jenny was married. I took a good hunk of the wedding-cake and put it under my pillow and kept it there five nights and never dreampt a thing. Then the sixth night I woke up about midnight feelin' kind o' hungry. so I ate it up"

CHARMS

.

LET a young woman pin a four-leaf clover over the door, and the first unmarried man who comes in the door will be the one she is to marry.

If, instead, the maiden prefers to eat the clover, or to put it in her shoe, she may recognize her fate in the first unmarried man she meets afterwards.

If you have lost your cow, catch a grandpa-long-legs, put a finger on one leg, and he will point with another leg in the direction in which you will find the stray cow.

Boy "That's so. They will tell you. Lots of times when I couldn't find a cow, I've just taken a grandpa-long-legs and he'd point just where it was Then I'd go that way and find it, when I couldn't find it no other way nohow."

Man "I've got a cow out here that'd trouble 'em some. The grandpa-long-legs d have to point in all directions to keep track of her "

If a grandpa-long-legs is not handy, spit in the palm of the left hand, strike the spittle with a finger of the right, and the direction the spittle jumps in will show what course to take in looking for the cow.

A good way to get rid of freckles is to go to a brook, catch a frog, and rub him alive on your face.

If you have too many rats in the house, take an old tin pan down cellar and give it a good drumming. The rats will hasten off the premises.

Possess yourself with a four-leaf clover and a stick with a knot-hole in it when you are to witness a sleight-of-hand performance. If aught puzzles you, there is need only to witness it through the knot-hole to have the trick made clear as day to you.

If your ear burns, it is a sign that somebody is talking about you. By wetting your thumb and forefinger and rubbing your ear, you can put a stop to the talk about you. If it is the right ear which burns, some one is saying something good of you. If the left ear burns, some one is saying something bad of you. In the latter case you will do well to pinch your ear, for that will make the

person who is talking about you bite
his tongue.

Repeat the Lord's Prayer backwards,
and you will see the Devil.

If you wish to get rid of the rats
which make the walls of your house
their home, write them a note couched
in the politest terms you are master of,
requesting them to go to a neighbor,
and they will do as you desire. Be
careful, of course, to tell the rats which
neighbor you wish them to go to

Another method, equally good, is to
catch a rat, carry it to a neighbor's, and
let it loose there. All the other rats at
your house will follow it.

Again, if you will catch a rat and let
it loose with a bell tied to its neck, all
the rats will leave.

If you get a fishbone in your throat,
pull your big toe, and the fishbone will
immediately come out.

In the old days when feruling was
common in the schools, the boys had a
belief that if they spit in their hand
before the teacher struck it, the ferule
would break in two at the first blow.

Once in a while there is a rare person who is endowed by nature with the
power to discover where it is best to

dig a spring or a well. This person, if you employ him, walks about your premises with a branch of witch-hazel in his hand At such spots as water can be struck without deep digging, the hazel branch droops downward, even if the medium attempts to prevent its doing so. By the way the twig twists and turns can be determined the exact spot where it will be best for you to dig.

A witch-hazel crotch is the favorite instrument of the water-finders. But there is a variation in preference Some claim it doesn't matter what sort of a tree the crotch comes from One old man I heard of used an apple-tree crotch. He demonstrated that he could locate waterpipes at the farm where he worked with no previous knowledge of where they were Every time he came over a pipe the crotch bent downward He really was able to tell just where the pipes were in spite of their crooked curves He was a simple, mild old laborer, and was not to be suspected of sleight of hand He said he couldn't prevent the downward inclination of the crotch if he tried to, but had no explanation to offer of the queer performance of the twig in his hand

One man gifted with this water-finding power is a minister. It is his idea that this is not a special gift, but that all of us have it He once followed back an underground watercourse to where another watercourse branched away from it. Here a well was dug that gave a most plenteous and never-failing supply of water He said that by careful calculation a person could determine how deep the water lay. For instance, notice the inclination of the crotch and the spot where the pull of the water first asserts itself. Then discover the spot that brings you right over it. A calculation can be made from the angle and the distance from the place where the pull was first felt that will show just how much digging is necessary.

A water-finder who uses an elm crotch says any one can find water in this way who has warm hands This man was something of a professional, and his charge was three dollars for each time he was employed

He says he has never failed but once in his water searching, and that was when the man didn't dig where he told him to.

After he made this statement, he was
employed one dry season to locate a
spring on a hillside in a village several
miles from his home

The crotch he used was long and
limber; and he wound the ends about
his palms, and grasped them very tight.
His palms were turned upward, and the
stick stood up vertically in the air above
them When he came over water the
top tipped outward and downward.   The
spot where it went down farthest was
the place where the best spring was.
Where there was water the crotch would
go down, even if he tried to prevent it
Sometimes the downward pull was so
forcible that when he held the twigs
tight the bark would be twisted off in
his hands He said that water in a
brook or in a pail did not affect the
mystic crotch ; the water must have dirt
over it to make the stick turn.

In the case I speak of the water-
finder went over the premises, and the
crotch indicated a spot in the corner of
a cornfield as the best one for a spring.
The man said there was a spring there
and a good one, only they would have
to dig twelve feet to strike it.

The corn was cut, and three men

spent two days digging a great circular
hole sixteen feet deep They failed to
find water. The elm-crotch man was
informed, and he came and looked down
the hole. He said he couldn't understand it. Then he saw yellow stains in
some of the dirt, and said there was iron
ore there, and it was that that had
attracted his wand.

"There's more'n one way to find a
spring," said man number one   "They
say you'll always find water where there's
ants. '

"Guess you'd find it in our buttery,
then," said man number two.

FORTUNE-TELLING

. .

FIND a daisy; ask it any question you please that can be answered by "Yes" or "No," and then, one at a time, pull off the petals. For the first say "Yes," for the second, "No," and so on. The word that falls to the last one is your answer.

Have you white marks on your nails? Put your hands together and say this rhyme while in succession you· touch finger-tips, beginning with the thumbs:—

A friend,
A foe,
A gift,
A beau,
A journey to go.

48

Notice on which finger-nails the marks are, and you will thus gain some inkling of your fortune.

Some authorities, however, say that the number of white marks on the nails indicate the number of lies the possessor has told.

"Oh, what a mess of lies!" comments one child, who notes numerous marks on a mate's nails. If the unhappy possessor of the marks complains to her mother, she is probably told not to mind, as the white blotches are only spots where she has hit the nails in some way.

CHARACTERS IN EYES

First form : —

> Gray eyes, greedy;
> Blue eyes, beauty;
> Black eyes, pig-a-pies,
> Sure to tell lies

Second form : —

> Black eyes, tell lies;
> Blue eyes, pick pies;
> Gray eyes, greedy gut,
> Eat all the world up.

Third form . —

> Blue eyes, pick pies,
> Turn around and tell lies,

Gray eyes, greedy gut,
Eat all the world up.

Children frequently tell fortunes on
their buttons. A boy will find out what
his station in life will be, and a girl the
kind of person she is to marry, by telling
them off, one button at a time, and saying this lingo over and over till the last
one is reached : —

"Rich man, poor man, beggar-man,
  thief,
Doctor, lawyer, merchant, chief."

To know what kind of clothes you are
to wear, you say, "Silks, satins, calico,
rags," over and over down to the last
button.

To know what kind of a vehicle you
are to ride in, you say, "Coach, carriage,
wheelbarrow, cart"

To know what kind of a creature will
draw your vehicle, you say, "Horse,
cow, pig, sheep."

To know what kind of a house you
will live in, you say, "Big house, little
house, pigpen, barn."

The list of possible residences sometimes runs in this form : "Palace, man-
sion, cottage, hut."

To know what kind of a wedding-ring

you will wear, you say, "Gold, silver, diamond, brass."

Instead of buttons you can, in this fortune telling, pull the petals off from a daisy, or the fronds one by one from a fern.

Children can tell the time of day by "dandelion clocks." Take a white-headed dandelion, blow it three times, and the number of seeds that still cling indicate the hour.

BIRTHDAY FORTUNES

Monday's child is fair of face,
Tuesday's child is full of grace,
Wednesday's child is sorry and sad,
Thursday's child is merry and glad,
Friday's child is loving and giving,
And Saturday's child must work for a
    living :
But the child that is born on the Sab-
    bath Day,
Is bonny and merry and glad and gay.

A rather more vigorous version is the following : —

Born on a Monday, fair of face ;
Born on a Tuesday, full of God's grace ;
Born on a Wednesday, merry and glad ;
Born on a Thursday, sour and sad ;

Born on a Friday, godly given ;
Born on a Saturday, work for a living ;
Born on a Sunday, never shall want ;
So there's the week and the end on't.

Some young people are fond of telling fortunes by naming an apple and
counting the seeds. At times this is
done at parties ; but the place may be
the back steps, or a seat on a convenient
fence. A companion snaps the apple to
be eaten with a forefinger, and, grant-
ing the eater is a girl, gives it the name
of some boy. When the apple is eaten
to the core, the apple-seeds are carefully
counted with this incantation : —

One, I love,
Two, I love,
Three, I love, I say ;
Four, I love with all my heart,
Five, I cast away.
Six, he loves,
Seven, she loves,
Eight, they both love,
Nine, he comes,
Ten, he tarries,
Eleven, he courts,
Twelve, he marries.

The sign which goes with the final

seed is, as matter of course, the one
which determines the character of the
fortune.

Pick a dandelion top that has gone
to seed Say, "Does my mother want
me?" and blow the white top with all
your might If all the seeds fly away,
your mother wants you right off If
they do not, keep on blowing The
number of blows it takes to clear the
dandelion head indicates in how many
hours your mother wants you.

"There was Grandmother Collins, she
used to tell fortins," said the old man I
was interviewing. "I recollect about
one girl that went to her. She said
that girl 'd have three beaux, and that
she'd marry the poorest one of the three
It all come out just as she'd said The
girl had three beaux, and she took and
married the worst one of the lot. Oh,
she got a miserable poor man for a husband. There'd be some nights she'd
sleep out in the cornfield, she was so
afraid of him

"There was some gypsies used to
come through here, and one of 'em was
an Injun woman. She was married to
one o' the men. She said she was full-
blooded Injun. She was a very pretty

lookin' woman, and she told fortins
You had to pay her a quarter. I give
her a quarter once, and she looked into
my hand, and said, 'You're goin to be
rich sometime,' and a lot of other stuff —
a gret long mess on it She didn't know
any more about fortins 'n I do, but she
'tended she did

"There is people can tell, though, and
tell it true. I was goin' down to Springfield, and I stopped at Cabotsville to see
Jim Tinkham that I'd always known for
a long time We was walking down a
street together when we come to a house
where we see a fat woman settin' in the
winder. Jim said she told fortins. He
said, 'Come in, and get your fortin told,
an' I'll pay the bill.'

"So we went in   Jim give the woman
a quarter, and she took a little grayish
stone, and begun to point out the spots
on't here and there along with her needle
She told me that on my way down I stopped in a house, and asked a young lady
for her company, 'And she give you the
mitten,' she said.

"Well, that was just as it had happened
to me   Then she told me about three
long journeys, one of 'em way out West
that I'd made   She told me everything

I ever did, and she described out my
farm better'n I could myself.

"I asked if I was ever goin' to get
married agin. She looked over her stone
and said, 'Here's lots of women I see.
Here's lots on 'em. You c'n have 'em
if you want 'em.'"

If at any time you want a yes or
no answer to some question, just get a
friend to gather the corners of a handkerchief up so that his hand is closed
over the ends, except a bit of the tips.
Then you take hold of two, and when
you straighten the handkerchief out if
you have got it the long way the answer is "yes"; if the short way, "no."

Take an apple, and pare it round and
round so that the skin will come off in
one continuous strand. Swing the paring around your head three times, and
then throw it over your shoulder. It
will, when it falls, take the form of some
letter of the-alphabet, or it ought to.
That letter will be the initial of your
beau's last name. If the initial won't
fit the last name of any person you consider attractive, those who practise this
art will allow you to try to make it fit
some one's first name. On account of the
curliness of the paring, the rounded let-

ters, and in particular S, occur oftenest. However, the letters are seldom so distinct but that an imaginative person can make something satisfactory to himself or herself out of the paring. Some say that it is important that the apple used in this divination should be a red one.

Pull a hair from your head, and give it to a friend. Next clasp your hands with your forefingers upright and touching tips. Then get your friend to draw the hair down between these two finger-tips For the first time the hair goes through say "a," for the second time "b," and so on through the alphabet until the hair breaks. The letter it breaks on is the initial of the one you are to marry. You can make your fortune much as you choose in this; for you have only to press your fingers tightly when you come to the letter that suits you, and the hair will break on that letter.

Eat the blossoms of three innocents, and the next person of the opposite sex that you meet will be the one you are to marry.

Squeeze the yellow centre off from a daisy stem, throw it into the air, and catch what you can of it when it comes down. Now take the pieces you caught, and say a letter of the alphabet for each one, beginning with a, b, c   The letter that comes on the final piece is the initial of the last name of the person who will some day marry you.

If a girl cuts thick slices of bread, it is a sign she will be a good stepmother.

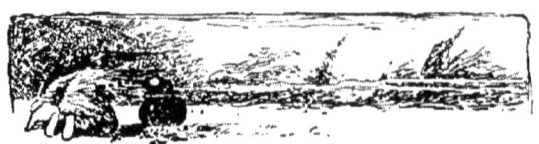

ODDS

. .

To cut the finger-nails on Sunday morning is a sign you will do something you are ashamed of before the week is out.

An old rhyme has it : —

It is better you were never born,
Than on the Sabbath pare hair or horn.

There is a finger-nail jingle for the days of the week : —

Cut them on Monday, cut them for
    wealth,
Cut them on Tuesday, cut them for
    health,
Cut them on Wednesday, cut them for
    news,
Cut them on Thursday, a new pair of
    shoes,
Cut them on Friday, cut them for woe,
Cut them on Saturday, a journey to go,
Cut them on Sunday, cut them for evil,
And be all the week as cross as the
    Devil.

Whistle to keep your courage up In
particular it is well to whistle when in
the night you have to go along a lonely
roadway.

Formerly many people were afraid to
pass a graveyard after nightfall for fear
of seeing ghosts. This fearsome feeling
has not entirely faded out even yet

When the Devil comes among human-
kind, he is fondest of taking the form of
a black cat, but at times a black dog
suits his purposes better It is said,
too, that he is pleased on occasion to
exhibit himself in the shape of a black
pig on the ridgepole of a house.

Professor Charles Eliot Norton remembers that when he was a boy he, with
some companions, met a woman whom
the others told him was a witch. They
said that if a knife was stuck in one of
her footprints it would make her turn
and look back One of the boys got out
his knife, and thrust the blade into one
of the woman's footprints. The little
company turned their eyes half fearfully
toward the witch's receding figure, but
for some reason or other she failed to
look around

Pass me salt, pass me sorrow.

It used to be taken as a pretty sure

sign that a man was conceited if he went about with his hat-brim turned up in front.

To use the side of the thimble instead of the tip to push the needle with is the sign of a good sewer.

It is well to have a piece of a branch cut from a mountain-ash in the house. It is as good to keep out witches as a horseshoe nailed over the door.

When a house burns, and another is built on the same spot, that, too, will burn soon.

Just so many stitches as you take on you,
Just so many lies you'll have told about
   you.

To "take stitches on you" is to repair a garment that you are wearing at the time you do the sewing.

Always pick up a pin with its head toward you; for that will insure your having a ride soon.

When you churn, turn the crank straight forwards all the time. If you turn it backwards, you will undo your work and soon bring the contents of the churn back to cream again.

Wet your finger and hold it above your head, and it will show you which way the wind blows. It will feel coolest, and will dry quickest, on the side whence the wind comes.

If you wipe at the same time on the same towel with another person, it is a sign you two will quarrel

" I don't believe half of these things they say are true "

If you have a scratch on the back of your hand, and it points toward your thumb, it is a sign you are going to have a ride If the scratch is a long one, the ride will be long, if short, the ride will be short.

Also : —

Nearer the thumb,
Sooner it'll come.

If the bottom of your foot itches, you may know that you are to step on strange lands

When a spark forms on the end of the wick in the candle-flame, moisten the tip of your finger with your tongue, touch the spark lightly with it, and if it adheres to your finger, you can confidently look for a letter within a day or two.

If you put on both stocking and shoe on one foot before putting on the stocking on the other foot, it is the sign that you are to meet with an accident.

Sing before breakfast, cry before supper.

If your nose itches, you may know that you are going to quarrel. Others have it that this is a sign you are going to get mad.

Pull out a hair, touch it with the flame of a match, and if it curls up quickly it is a sign you are cross in your disposition. Instead of using fire. you can, if you choose, pull the hair between a finger and the thumb nail to discover whether it will curl up quickly or not.

Pull out a gray hair, and ten or twelve will come in its place.

If you pull one of your fingers, and the joint cracks, it is a sign you have told a lie.

Broad finger-nails indicate generosity. Long finger-nails indicate a lack of thrift.

If you go out visiting on Monday, it is a sign you will go out visiting every day that week.

On the inner side of a horse's legs is a horny scab about the size of a dollar. It used to be said that flakes from this made excellent bait for fishing.

A sore on the tip of the tongue is a sign you have told a lie.

If a person's front teeth are far apart, it is a sign that person is going to be a wanderer.

Put the wrong foot out of bed first when you get up in the morning, and you will be cross all day. Always get up right foot foremost

If you take hold of a chair, and twist it about on one leg, it is a sign you are going to quarrel

When we have one fire in town, there's always three in a short time

> Wash and wipe together,
> Live in peace forever.

Bright red auroras were formerly said to be the sign that a great battle had been fought, or was soon to be fought. Its flaming streamers betokened blood and slaughter There was this fiery omen in the sky at the time of the battle of Bunker Hill, and other contests of the Revolution, as well as of the older French and Indian wars.

Often when two persons make a bargain they at its conclusion " Shake hands on it " to make it binding

When you get up in the morning be

sure to dress your right foot first. If you don't, you will meet with a disappointment that day.

When a girl asked her mother on which side she should make the buttonholes in a garment she was making, the mother would respond, " Always make them on the left side   Remember this, that you don't want to be on the buttonhole side of heaven, and you won't have to ask again." This refers to the parable wherein the goats were divided from the sheep, and went to the left of the throne

In haying time, if you can "step your shadow," it is noon   This means that you must be able to step on the shadow of your head   You cannot do this in northern countries except on summer noons when shadows are short.

Step over the graves in the cemetery or go around them. If you walk on them, woe will come to you in some form

If you eat crumbs 'twill make you wise,
If you leave the crust
You're sure to bust

This is schoolboy poetry recited to a mate who, in eating his lunch, throws away the crust

"There's a good deal of pizen in people, especially in red-headed men. All folks hev some, but there's more pizen in a red-headed man than in a man that has black hair — a good deal. In London, a red-headed man that was a sailor sold himself to a doctor for quite a sum of money.

"The doctor strung him up by his heels, and put a toad at his mouth, and the man died, and a great lot of green, nasty-looking pizen oozed out that the doctor said was very valuable."

Drop a dish of victuals, and you will hear bad news.

Grass will not grow under a "gallus" where a man has been hung.

Sneeze on Monday, sneeze for danger,
Sneeze on Tuesday, kiss a stranger,
Sneeze on Wednesday, sneeze for a let-
    ter,
Sneeze on Thursday, for something
    better,
Sneeze on Friday, sneeze for sorrow,
Sneeze on Saturday, see your sweet-
    heart to-morrow,
Sneeze on Sunday, your safely seek.
The Devil 'll have you the rest of the
    week.

When a child gets dizzy whirling, he needs only to whirl in the opposite direction to turn himself back to stability.

When you comb your hair, don't burn such as gathers on your comb. If you do, it will make you cross.

Don't have any metal about you when there is a thunder-storm. It will draw the lightning, and you will like enough get struck. The boys who understand this take care not to have a jacknife or any such thing on their persons in thunder-storms, and some women when they hear the storm's muttering approach take off their rings, hide the scissors, and cover the sewing-machine. There are those who shut the blinds, and draw the curtains to keep out sight and sound, and then lie down on a feather bed to wait for the storm to pass.

If the back of your legs itch, you may know that you are to go on a long journey.

When you play hi-spy, and are "it," and want to know where the others have hid, take a stick and put it up on end and let it fall. If it falls three times in the same direction, that shows you the way to go to find the hiders.

After you have had a tooth pulled out, don't touch the cavity with your tongue, and the next tooth that comes will be a gold tooth.

When you move to a new house always send beforehand a loaf of bread and a new broom.

Sneeze early and you will hear some news, or get a present that same day

Button your coat wrong, or draw on a stocking inside out, and matters will go crooked that day

Rock an empty cradle, and you will injure the child that usually sleeps in it.

When, in pitching up hay, your fork gets caught and taken up on the load, you have lost a day's work. That is, your work won't amount to anything that day, or else you'll never get any pay for it

Drop your hoe or your rake, and you will likewise lose a day's work.

Talk to yourself, and you talk to the Devil.

If the basting-threads are in a garment, that is a sign it is not paid for

It is a sign a man's clothes are not paid for if the little size cards are still on them.

It is a good sign to take out your work; that is, if you have to pull out your stitches because you have made a

mistake.   It proves that you will live to
wear the garment out.

Do you want to know whether you
love butter or not?   Get some one to
hold a buttercup under your chin   If
they can see a yellow reflection from its
burnished petals on your chin, then you
do love butter.   If not, you don't.

Stumpy fingers are a sign that one
must work for a living

You can get a hundred dollars for a
million old postage-stamps   I never
heard that any one got that many, nor
can I find out who is going to pay the
hundred dollars, but a good many young
people in the cities have made up their
minds to collect the million stamps.
They are most successful when they or
their friends can pick over the letters
that come to offices or stores   I suppose if one could average a hundred
stamps every week-day the year through,
he would be doing pretty well.   At that
rate, if the collector persevered, he
would get his million stamps in about
thirty years.   If he spent ten minutes
a day soaking off, drying, and caring
for the stamps, he would in that length
of time put in three hundred full days
of ten hours each.   When he received

his hundred dollars, he would therefore be paid for his time at the rate of thirty-three and one-third cents a day

When the bars of the northern lights shoot up in a cone shape, like guns stacked, that is a sure sign of war.

If you want the cake you make to be light, stir the batter only one way

Hemlock-trees attract lightning. It is said that you need put no lightning-rods on your buildings if you will only set up a tall hemlock pole near them The lightning will hit that pole, rather than the buildings, every time.

All sound-minded people have the largest half of their heads in front of their ears. A man with the heaviest part of his head back of his ears you may be pretty sure is an idiot.

Sleep before midnight is "beauty sleep." Therefore if you wish to be handsome go to bed early.

FRIENDS

GAIN a day, and you gain a friend, as, for instance, when it is Thursday and you think it is Friday. Lose a day, and you lose a friend.

Never give a friend a pin It will spoil your friendship. To guard against this, and at the same time to accommodate your friend, you can say " I will not give you the pin, but I will lend it to you for ninety-nine years.'

When a friend leaves you, don't watch the friend out of sight, for the person who is watched out of sight will never be seen by you again if you do.

When you and a companion are walking together, don't allow a third person to go between you. If you do, it will cut your friendship. Nevertheless, if, in spite of precautions, this should happen, say, " Bread and butter," and the fates will be propitiated.

Nor should you, when walking with a friend, let a tree separate you. If this occurs, the best thing to do is for one of you to retrace your steps, and come past the tree on the side your friend took.

Don't make a friend a present of a knife; for, according to every authority versed in sign lore, if you do, it will cut your friendship. All sharp-edged tools are equally unfitted as presents for the same reason.

"There was Sue Perkins, years ago, and Harry Wright was keepin' company with her. One day he gave her a pair of scissors. They was beautiful scissors too. Some of 'em told her not to take 'em, and said it would cut their friendship. But she said she didn't care anything about their signs. 'We sha'n't have any trouble between us. I know we won't,' she said. But I'll be blamed if they didn't have a row inside of a month, and Harry Wright stopped callin', and Sue Perkins lived and died an old maid."

WISHES

. .

If for seven consecutive nights you can see one star before any others are in sight, and will repeat this rhyme each time without saying anything to any one, you can make any wish you choose and it will come true.

Star light, star bright,
First star I see to-night;
I wish I could, I wish I might
Have the wish I wish to-night.

Others say this when they see the first star : —

Star light, star bright,
The first I've seen to-night,
I wish — I wish —

Then they tell what they wish.

Still others say —

The first star bright I've seen to-
    night,
May I see somebody I don't expect
    to see.

The first form of this wish has to be
repeated three times.

When you see the first robin in the
spring, wish, and your wish will come to
pass In this, as in all wishing-spells,
you must be careful not to tell any one
If you do, the first robin will be quite
ineffectual as an aid to the realization
of wishes. You must be careful also
not to speak until you have wished, for
that too, will break the spell   " I
wished on robins for a good many years.
There's no harm in wishing, you know,
if you wish good wishes "

Wish on the first frogs you hear in
the spring, tell no one, and the wish will
come true

Notice the white horses that pass,
count them up to three, and shake hands
with somebody Then you can make a
wish, and it will come true

The forked bone just in front of the
breast-bone of a chicken or other fowl is
known as the wish-bone If this bone

chances to fall to you, preserve it, and
put it on the shelf behind the stove to
dry. When properly seasoned you take
hold of one end, let a friend take hold
of the other, each make a wish, and
then both pull. The wish of the one
that has the top with his piece when it
breaks will come true.

Find a white-headed dandelion, make
a wish, and then try to blow the seeds
off with one breath. If the seeds all
leave at one blow, your wish will come
true. Otherwise it will not.

MEDICINAL

. .

WHEN you have the rheumatism, carry a potato in your pocket. The potato will become hard after a time, and believers in its virtues affirm that this is because of the rheumatism it has absorbed.

Eat poison ivy, and it will never poison you afterward. When this remedy is mentioned, the comment usually is, "Well, I guess it wouldn't. You wouldn't live to give it the chance."

When a child has fits, the parents sometimes get a puppy for the child to play with and sleep with. The belief is that the dog will take the disease, and that as the dog grows worse the child will grow better. When the dog dies, the child will be completely cured.

Carry a horse-chestnut in your pocket and you will not be troubled by rheumatism.

The child that wears a black silk cord around its neck will not have the croup

The black silk cord so worn is likewise good to keep off the diphtheria.

If a young person sleeps with an elderly person the latter will weaken the former by drawing vitality from the young person. The elder is not supposed to get any benefit from the fact.

Prick a sty with a pricker off a gooseberry bush, and it will get well at once.

Rub a sty with a wedding-ring, and it will go off.

Pull an eyewinker from the sty, and that will be the end of it.

Some prefer to make sure of a sty's leaving by touching it with the tail of a black cat.

INDIAN MAGIC.

In ye olden time one of the farmers at Hadley, Mass., had the misfortune to cut his foot while chopping in the woods. Moreover, the wound was so grievous it refused to heal. Neither the home poultices nor the doctor's lotions had any effect, and the man began to fear that these were his last days. While things were thus, going from bad to worse, an Indian woman heard of the case, and offered to heal the man's wound. Her services were accepted, and she asked

for the axe which made the cut. When
it was given to her, she did the axe-helve
up carefully in salve, and the man's
wound got well right off.

Wear a red string around your neck
to keep off rheumatism

Carry an onion in your pocket, and
you will not have fits.

Carry camphor-gum, and you will not
catch small-pox or contagious diseases.

" I had a great-aunt that used to have
the cramp terrible till some one told her
to tie a cotton string around her ankle.
After that she never had a cramp to the
end of her days."

The gall of rattlesnakes used to be
thought excellent as a cure for bilious-
ness.

Wear an eelskin around your waist to
keep off rheumatism Some say they
had rather have the rheumatism.

Carry a piece of brimstone to keep
off the itch. Some people carry it to
keep off scarlet fever and other contagious diseases Others wear a little bag
of sulphur hung by a string around the
neck There are those who carry a
lump of sulphur in their pocket, and
they will get it out and sniff it vigor-
ously when they think themselves in
danger

If a bald-headed man washes his head with sage tea, it will make a new growth of hair come out

The use of tobacco is believed to prevent one's taking diseases

The sick person that shows an inclination to stretch will get well.

If a sick person itches, he will get well

If he is cross, he will get well

"That isn't always so. There was a man in our town who was very sick, and his wife did something or other he didn't like, and he sat right up in bed and swore at her, and the next instant he fell over dead."

Put the first aching tooth you have pulled in a glass of whiskey. Then drink the whiskey, and you will never have occasion to have another tooth pulled because it aches

Carry an onion with you to keep off diseases. You can't take a disease from any odor that the onion scent is strong enough to overcome so that you don't smell it. Indeed, whatever you can't smell won't harm you, onion or no onion. But if you think you smell a disease, even if you don't, you are liable to have that disease.

A good way to keep from having cramps is to wear an eelskin around your ankle.

Read gravestone epitaphs, and you will lose your memory.

When you want to go to sleep and can't, count up to twenty-three hundred.

If that doesn't work, just imagine a crow flying round and round up in the sky in large circles.

Sleep with a piece of steel under your pillow, and you will not have the rheumatism. I have heard of one woman who always put her scissors under her pillow, when bedtime came, for this purpose

"Do you ever have the nightmare? Well, sir, my father used to have nightmare right along every night. He'd be all of a didder — shakin' and shudderin' till my mother'd take hold of him and wake him up. That'd bring him right out of 'em.

"One time he went away from home, and it come night and they was sittin' around in the tavern bar-room, and he told one o' the men there that he really dreaded to go to bed He told him how he always had the nightmare, and how, bein' away from home, he wouldn't have

his wife to wake him up He said he
was afraid he might die in it

"'Well,' says the man, 'I'll tell you a
cure for that; and if it don't work when
you try it to-night, I'll stand drinks for
the crowd in the mornin' If it does
work, you c'n stand the drinks '

"There was fifteen or twenty men
there; but father agreed, for he knew if
he got a sure cure for those nightmares,
it'd be worth it

"So the man says, 'Now, when you
go to bed, you just smell your stock-
in's after you take 'em off That's all
you've got to do, and you won't have no
nightmare to-night, I'll warrant you.'

"Father did it, and it was just as the
man said Now, if any of your friends
have the nightmare, you want to tell
'em of that, and they'll thank ye for it
when they've found out how sure it
cures 'em "

If your right nostril bleeds. you can
stop it by tying a cord tight around your
left little finger If it is your left nostril
that bleeds, tie the cord around the right
little finger

" My brother used to be quite a hand
to have cramps. Finally some one told
him that when he had 'em he must wet

his finger, and make a cross right on the calf of his leg. He done it, and it cured him every time. He says he don't know of anything better'n that for cramps."

Wear a piece of red woollen yarn around your neck, and it will keep you from having the nosebleed. " My brother had to do that."

If you have a sore throat, tie one of the stockings you have worn through the day around your neck when you go to bed. The sore throat can't stand that, and will have left by morning. The stocking should be tied on with the hollow of the foot next to the throat.

Some people keep themselves from taking contagious diseases by wearing a silver piece on a string around their neck. When, presently, the silver piece turns black, they know the silver has done good work in absorbing diseases that otherwise might have killed them. From a physician's point of view, however, this black on the coin is the effect on the silver of the sulphur in the secretions of the skin.

A good many people have an idea that a person enjoys better health, and lives longer, if he is in the habit of sleeping with his head to the north. The important point is not that the head is to the north, but that the electric pole is in that direction.

Some people prefer to sleep with the head to the east   It is in that direction that the earth turns, and they think it healthier to be projected through space head first

Wear a tarred string around your neck to keep you from taking contagious diseases.

If you want to go to sleep and can't, just imagine two hundred sheep going through some bars one at a time   Count 'em up slow, and it will put you to sleep sure before you get to the last one.   It takes your mind, you see.

Trim your finger-nails on Friday, and you will not have the toothache for a week.

Eat pudding and milk, and it will make your hair curl.   If it suits your taste better, you can eat crusts of bread, for that, too, will make your hair curl.

You can stop another person's bleeding by touching the cut, bruise, or whatever it is, with your finger, and saying, "I bequeath thee not to bleed, not to fester, not to canker, nor to swell, but to heal.   In the name of God, amen."

You need not say this aloud unless you choose. The bleeding will stop at once. This works on animals as well as people.

If your eyes are weak, have your ears bored just as you would for earrings That will help make your eyes strong.

You can cure another person's headache by rubbing the aching one's head. The headache will presently leave the sufferer, and you will have it yourself, but less severely. A rheumatic shoulder treated in the same way brings the same results.

"I don't like to believe in presentiments and things of that sort, but I do have spells of believing. It's mostly your imagination that's queer, though. There was a fellow once that worked in a mill in Holyoke, and the fellows got hold of his hat one morning and tightened the band. Then they told him his head was swollen dreadfully.

"He didn't think so; but they got him to try on his hat, and it wouldn't go on. They said he looked sick, and he looked in the glass and said he believed he did look sick; he hadn't thought of it before, and he went home feeling pretty badly off."

Soon after the war, it was discovered

by one of our American physicians that
certain rays from the sun possessed
marked curative qualities. The blue
rays, in particular, had remarkable virtues. This gave rise to what was known
as " The blue glass craze.' For a few
months a great deal was published in
the papers on the subject, and it was
a common topic of conversation. People had blue panes of glass put into
their windows, or they covered their window panes with blue tissue for the light
to fall through. Some had glas summer-
mer-houses made all in blue, and lived in
them much of their time. Others made
blue glass sanitariums of the upper story
of their houses by putting in blue sky-
lights

Many marvellous cures were effected,
but the agitation and the interest in the
matter passed away as quickly as does
a summer day's thunder-storm. It was
claimed that a sunbath under this blue
glass was good for diseases of all kinds,
and that blue glass was also good to
assist vegetation In fact, the believers
in its virtues used it over their hotbeds.

THE FARM

. .

IF the sun shines through the limbs of the apple-trees on Christmas Day, there will be a good crop of fruit next year.

Plant a bean with the eye up, and it will grow straight down through the earth to China.

When you have a kettle of fat pork on the stove that you are trying down into lard, and want to know if it is done, put a match into it. If the match lights, the lard is done. If it doesn't light, keep on cooking your lard.

When you have land to clear up, chop the trees and cut the brush "when the sign is in the heart," and you will be sure to kill these growths.

If you have a tree that bears no fruit, put a stone in its first crotch just before blossoming-time. The tree will surely be fruitful after that.

Great was the belief at one time
among the farmers in plaster as a fer-
tilizer. Vast quantities were sowed on
the land. It was affirmed that its power
was such that if you used it in a field
next to that of a neighbor who did not,
it would draw his manure right over the
fence. To-day plaster is a thing of the
past, and the farmer questions if he ever
got any particular benefit from its use.

There are now few farmers who have
a regular habit of soaking their wagon-
wheels, but it is not difficult to find
those who, when on a journey, take
such opportunities as offer themselves
along the road to give their wheels a
wetting. The object is to make the
wood swell, and keep the spokes from
rattling and the wheels themselves from
tumbling to pieces. On country roads
there is once in a while a place where
at one side of a bridge that crosses a
little brook is a track by which you can
drive down and through the water. If
you take this side path and ford the
stream, you can accomplish three objects, — wet your wheels, water your
horse, and soak the horse's hoofs. But
the farmer who wants to do the soaking
thoroughly stops at every wayside wa-

tering trough, and pours a few pailfuls over his wheels.

Years ago a farmer who was going on a long trip would, the night before, sometimes set his wheels in the long log watering-trough in the barnyard, and turn them occasionally to make the soaking complete. In Europe farmers, on the evening before a journey, have been known to throw their wheels into a pond, when one was handy, and leave them over night.

A New England farmer who took this method of soaking the wheels of one of his old wagons had them all carried off by one of the town deacons who thought they had been thrown away.

The general effect on the wheels of this soaking process is to keep them expanding and shrinking. The temporary effect is all right, but in the end decay and decrepitude are hastened.

LUCK

To find a horse-shoe in the road is a sign of good luck. Many of the poorer farm-houses of New England have a horseshoe tacked up over an outer entrance for good luck.

In times past, and those not very far removed, the object of the horseshoe over the door was to keep out the witches.

The horseshoe should be put up with the curve downward. If the open end is down, all your luck will run out.

Carry a lucky-bone, and nothing will harm you. This bone is from the head of a codfish. It is shell-like and narrow,

with a length of three-fourths of an inch
The edge is notched, and the color is a
pearly white — very pretty.

It is a good plan to carry two lucky-
bones. That will make your luck doubly
sure. They should be both from the
head of the same fish.

When you drop your bread and butter and it falls butter-side down, bad
luck is not very far off. There are
those that affirm that the bread always
drops butter-side down.

When you move from one habitation
to another, don't take the cat with you.
Bad luck will follow if you do.

When you play cards and have bad
luck, get up and go around your chair.
A still easier way to turn your luck is
to blow in the cards.

When fishing, spit on your bait for
good luck. Certain of the most igno-
rant class will spit on money for good
luck.

When you start on an errand or a
journey, don't turn back, no matter what
you may have forgotten. If you do, ill
luck in some form will overtake you.

"Some people who get started, and
then think of something they've forgot
before they've got out of sight and hear-

ing of the house, will stand right there
and holler half an hour for some one to
fetch it, rather than go back."

> See a pin and let it lie,
> Come to sorrow by-and-by.

Another version is : —

> See a pin and let it lay,
> Want you will and want you may

Another couplet is · —

> See a pin and pick it up,
> All the day you'll have good luck.

Others repeat this rhyme : —

> See a pin and let it lie,
> Bad luck you'll have until you die,

Or · —

> You'll want that pin before you die.

It is a sign of good luck to fall up
hill.

It is unlucky to get out of bed on the
side opposite to the accustomed one.
The person who shows signs of cross-
ness is always liable to be reminded of
it by the remark, " Well, guess you got
out of the wrong side of your bed this
morning."

If a spider spins down from the ceiling toward you, he will bring you good luck.

If you trip up on something, it is a sign of bad luck. The best thing for you to do in such a case is to go back and walk it over.

If it is a stone you have fallen over, go back and touch it.

When a ring on the finger has been wished on, or was placed there by some one else, it will bring bad luck if you allow it to be removed

If, when you start on a journey, you forget something and have to return, sit down before you again start, or the journey will be unlucky.

If you put on your apron wrong side out, wear it so, or in making the change you will change your luck. This applies as well to the putting on of a stocking wrong side out, or any other article of apparel.

Some say that it is safe to right the garment if you take pains to ward off the impending woe by spitting on the garment. To do this genteelly, you need only to moisten the finger-tip with the tongue, and touch the wrong garment. Then you can turn the garment again and no harm will result.

If you spill your salt at the table, it is a sign you will quarrel with your best friend. You can break the compelling spell of this accident by throwing on the stove the salt that was spilled.

Others have it that spilling salt means simply bad luck, and that you can break the spell by throw a pinch of it over the left shoulder.

Along the shores of many of our streams live numerous families of water-bugs that have hard and shiny black backs, and that, when in motion, skim about on the surface with great activity. They are called "Lucky bugs," and it is well known among the boys that to catch one brings good fortune

When a pointed object you have thrown or dropped sticks up in the ground or floor, it is a sign of good luck.

The finding anything which has any value is a sign of good luck.

"My brother found a penny one day by the doorstep at the schoolhouse. He had good luck afterwards, but I've forgotten what 'twas."

The finding a penny is surer to bring you good luck than almost anything else. Don't spend it, but keep it, and carry it for a "lucky penny." It will bring you

good fortune ; but if you spend it, or lose
it, you will have bad luck, or, at any rate,
a sort of indifferent luck such as any one
might have.

If a strange dog or cat comes to you
and makes its home with you, it will
bring you good luck, and a black cat
brings its owner good luck

To carry a hoe into the house is a
sign of bad luck.

Be particular to put your right foot
foremost when you leave the house, or
ill luck will betide you.

Carry a large old-fashioned cent for a
"pocket piece." It will bring you good
luck.

A five-dollar gold piece is also supposed to be a lucky coin, and a bright
new penny has virtues in the same
line The former may be kept laid
away in a drawer to hand down as an
heirloom

If the first object you meet when you
start on a journey is a woman or a cat,
you will have bad luck before you return
If the woman is barefoot, it portends
such a degree of bad luck as makes it
best to turn back and not go that day

When you start on a journey, have a
care not to put your left arm into your

jacket first   Such a proceeding would bring ill luck.

When you take a piece of cake on your plate, and it tips over on its side, that is a sign of bad luck.

See that all the wedding-cake is eaten, for then the married pair will have good luck.

If an even number of crows flies overhead, it is a sign of bad luck.

Put on your vest wrong side out, and you will change your luck if you turn it right

Friday is an unlucky day, and it is therefore unwise to begin any work on that day.   Many people would not think of marrying, or starting on a journey, on the "Hangman's Day."

To have a hen crow is a sign of bad luck.

It is a sign of good luck to find a four-leaf clover.

When you are on a journey, and see a squirrel run across the road in front of you, note his direction   If he went across to the right, you will have good luck, if to the left, bad luck.

If you buy the materials for a new dress and do not make it up before you are married, you will have very bad luck

Spiders carry good luck with them.
Some people will not kill them for fear
of spoiling their luck.

If you find the cat sitting with her
tail to the fire, expect bad luck

You will have bad luck if when you
get out of bed you rise backwards.   You
should get up face forwards

There is luck in odd numbers.

There is, once in a while, a man who,
when he sneezes, says, " God bless it,"
that the sneeze may bring him good
luck   If he hears some one else sneeze,
he helps them to good luck by saying,
" God bless you."

— Don't pass under a ladder; it will
make you have bad luck

Rock an empty chair, and you will
bring bad luck

It is unlucky to meet a flock of sheep.

It is unlucky to meet a drove of pigs.

It is bad luck to turn over in bed
The boy who made this affirmation said
he had heard of two men who slept together, and who always woke up at midnight, and got out each on his side of
the bed, and ran around the foot and
got in on the other side.   Thus they
adjusted themselves to a new position
without turning over in bed.

SNAKES

. .

" THE way a snake catches birds and
frogs and things is not by chasing and
grabbing them, but by charming them.
It just gets its eyes on their eyes, and
runs its tongue out and in, and then
the bird can't move if it wanted to.
The snake keeps that up a while, and
then he can take his own time about
doin' the swallerin'. You have to be
kind o' careful yourself about not bein'
charmed, specially by black snakes.
I know there was some of the children
out berrying one time, and Sarah Hill
came near bein' charmed. They thought
she was comin' along all right, when they
noticed she warn't with 'em. They
ran back then, and Sarah was standin'

still lookin' right into a bush. They
told her to come along, and she didn't
say a word Then they tried to pull
her away, but she said, 'Don't,' because she saw such beautiful sights.
Well, there was a black snake in that
bush, and she was bein' charmed by it.
Little more'n she might a got bit."

When a snake proposes to charm you,
it looks you straight in the eye in such
a sinister and unwinking way that you
are fascinated and paralyzed

I was told the story of a boy who
was charmed one day His companions
found him looking at a snake and making a strange kind of noise He did
not come to himself until they killed
the snake, and broke the spell

An old farmer told me that one morning when he was out mowing his attention was attracted by a bird fluttering
around a bush in a queer kind of way.
" It was makin' sort of a mournful
noise, and flutterin' round and round
close to the bush I went along up to
the bush to see what the matter was
Then I see there was an adder in there
watching of it, and its nest was in that
bush. The snake was charming it, for
I no sooner give the bush a little shake

and took the snake's attention, than
away the bird went as quick as a flash

"I s'pose most any kind of a snake
will charm birds and such things, but
I don't s'pose these striped snakes
are powerful enough to charm people.
Black snakes and rattlers will, though
My uncle got charmed once. He was
goin' along through the woods with my
father when he stopped and was gettin'
left behind. My father called to him to
come along; but he didn't pay no attention — just kep' lookin' at somethin'
My father see he was gettin' charmed by
a snake. So he went back and give him
a yank, and then they killed the snake.
He said he wanted to come when father
called him, but he couldn't He said
that he saw everything that was pretty,
— all the colors he ever thought of and
more too, and they seemed to be right
in the snake's eyes."

Many still believe that in drinking
from brooks one runs the risk of swal-
lowing a young snake, which is liable to
grow in the stomach, and become large
and troublesome In support of this
idea, it is related that once there was a
certain child that took large quantities
of food, in particular a great deal of

milk, yet became more and more ema-
ciated One night when the child was
sitting at the table with a bowl of milk
before it, of which it had not eaten, a
great snake put its head out of the
child's mouth. Apparently it was hungry, had scented the milk, and came
up out of the child's stomach to get
it. The child's father was by, and he
gripped the snake by the neck, and
pulled it out It was four feet long

Some say that instead of a bowl of
milk on the table, it was a pailful on the
kitchen-floor fresh from the cow

Another telling of the story has it that
a woman swallowed the snake As it
grew she was in great distress, so that
finally she could not eat At length her
friends laid her down with her stomach
on a chair, and put a basin of steaming
hot food on the floor before her That
brought out the snake, and the woman
got well

It is bad enough to have a snake in
your stomach, but you are even worse
off if you meet with one of these hoop-
snakes Let one of those chase you,
and you are a goner They ain't afraid
of a man no more'n nothin', and they
can run faster'n any horse goin'. The

way the snake does is to pick its tail
up in its mouth, and then whirl over
and over like a hoop. His tail is sharp-
pointed and hard like a spike When
he catches up with you, he just takes
his tail out of his mouth, and jabs it into
you Oh, I tell you, you'd better swallow
a dozen snakes rather'n get one o' these
hoop-snakes after you

It is said that when a hoop-snake
strikes a man it "blasts" him I sup-

pose that means he is paralyzed, turns
black, shrivels up, and like enough
blows away When one of these hoop-
snakes strikes its tail into anything
wooden, — a hoe-handle, for instance, —
it shivers the wood into splinters, just
as if it had been struck by lightning

Another snake you want to beware of
is the "black racer snake" It is said

that he has a bluish tinge, and that he will chase a man whenever he gets sight of one.

Kill the first snake,
And break the first brake,
And you will conquer all you undertake.

That is, the first snake and the first brake seen in the spring.

Put a horse-hair in water, and it will turn into a snake. This superstition has two facts behind it which give it a semblance of truth. Firstly, a horse-hair put in water will twist and curl quite curiously. Secondly, there is a kind of worm sometimes seen in stagnant pools which strongly resembles a coarse horse-hair.

Cut a snake's tail off, and the tail will not die until the sun goes down. The basis of this saying is that it is a fact that the tail will continue to wriggle and show signs of life long after it is separated from the body.

Some authorities affirm that you can cut a snake all to pieces, and its parts will not cease to move till the end of the day.

If, after cutting a snake in two, you put the parts into water, they will unite into a whole snake again.

Most persons who meet a snake either
run off or try to kill it. Many snakes
are known to be harmless, and even
useful. People kill them because they
are unpleasant looking creatures, and
because it is the fashion. But besides,
there is an inherited and underlying
reason, which is that it is understood
that God put a curse on snakes in the
Bible, and has commanded that they be
killed.

"I've hearn 'em tell about how that
there was a little girl once that always
used to eat her dinner out-doors when it
was good weather. She'd get her plate
full, and then she'd go off out back o'
the barn somewhere, and nobody didn't
know what she went off like that for. So
after a while her folks followed her; and
she went along out there by a stone wall
and set down, and she rapped on her
plate, and out there come a big rattlesnake, and went to eatin' off the plate
with her. And when the snake got over
on to her side of the plate too much,
she'd rap him with her spoon, and push
him away, and say, " Keep back, Gray-
coat, on your own side." Her folks
didn't like to have her eatin' with a
snake that way, and they sent her off

to stay somewhere else. When she was
gone, they went and killed the snake.
Bimeby the little girl come home again,
and then she found out her snake was
killed. Arter that she kind o' pined
away and died.

"I've hearn 'em tell about that a good
many times, and I s'pose that's a pretty
true story."

THE POWLR OF IRISH EARTH

"ST PATRICK, as is well known, ban-
ished all snakes from Ireland some hun-
dreds of years ago There isn't a snake
in the whole country — they can't live
there. You may take a snake into Ireland in a big bottle, and as long as
you keep the cork in, he's all right,
but let him breathe the air, or let him
touch the earth or water anywhere in
Ireland, I don't care where, and he's
a dead man in less'n no time.

"Why, there was an Irishman made a
bet with an American in Boston, that
if he made a ring of Irish earth around
a snake, the snake couldn't get out of it
He bet seven hundred dollars, because
that was all he had. Then he went
over to Ireland, and got a little bag of
sand from the shore near Dublin When

he got back here, he made a circle with
it on the ground, and they put a snake
inside the circle. The snake couldn't
get over that ring to save himself, and
the divil died there, and the man got his
seven hundred dollars."

FOLKS

. .

A poor man always keeps a dog, and a very poor man keeps two.

Red-headed people are usually quick-tempered, or, in other words, "spunky."

The baby who doesn't fall down-stairs before it is a year old will turn out a fool.

Likewise the baby must fall out of bed three times before it is a year old, or it won't know anything

The boy who goes through a door with a hoe over his shoulder will never grow taller.

Insane persons were thought in days not very remote to be possessed of evil spirits.

Idiots were thought to be peculiarly under the care of the Deity, and it was believed that those who treated them kindly would be blessed.

When you see a woman stirring her batter from left to right, you may know she is a good cook. If she stirs from right to left, that is a sign she is a poor cook.

It will make a child proud if you let it look in a mirror before it is twelve months old.

The person whose second toe is longer than his great toe is born to rule. If the person with such a toe is a woman, she says she knows by that she will rule her husband ; or, as one woman put it, "It's a sign I'm going to fight with my old man all my days."

If three persons of the same first name come together, you may be pretty sure one of them is a fool.

"When a man goes to sit down in a chair, he always takes hold of its back and moves it. Perhaps he won't move it more'n an inch or two, but ninety-nine cases out of a hundred he will move it a little. When a woman goes to sit down, she sits down in the chair just where it was. If men and women dressed exactly alike, you could tell 'em apart that way if you couldn't no other. Now, you notice that."

A person with very light hair will have poor eyes.

A person with prominent eyes is sure to be a great talker.

MONEY

. .

EARLY to bed and early to rise
Makes a man healthy, wealthy,
and wise.

When you see a shooting star, if
you can say, " Money before the
week's out," three times over before it is lost to sight, you will
have some money before the week
is out.

If you see a man going about
with his hat brim turned up behind,
you may know that he has money to
let. Others say it is a sign that the
man likes cider.

It is a sign you are going to be rich
if you tumble up-stairs.

If your eyebrows grow together, you
either are rich or are going to be. You
may be even surer of this coming true
if your eyebrows are bushy. You notice
the rich men that you know, and you'll
find that they nearly every one have
bushy eyebrows that grow together.

107

When you see a man with one pant leg in his boot and the other out, you may know that he has money to let.

If a man has to wear out his wedding clothes, he will never get rich.

It is a sign that a person is going to be wealthy if he picks up all the pins he finds   There is logic in this, in that it indicates a saving disposition.

A scratch on the hand is a sign of money.

When making pies, if the person engaged in the work, after putting the crust on the plate, trims it all around without changing hands, it is a sure sign she will be wealthy.

If the palm of your left hand itches, it is a sign that money is coming to you soon.   Have a care about scratching it, for that will break the enchantment.

But if you will —

Rub it on three kinds of wood,
'Twill come to good

Carry a dice in your pocketbook, and you will always have money

The woman who sews between daylight and dark will always be poor. Others have it that the woman who sews at that time will make her husband poor.

The way in which one's shoes wear
out will indicate one's habits in spend-
ing money.

> Wear at the toe,
> Spend as you go.
> Wear at the heel,
> Spend a good deal
> Wear at the ball,
> Spend all

If it is a girl or unmarried woman
who studies her shoes for omens, she
may add another couplet

> Wear at the side,
> A rich man's bride

There was a time in the earlier half
of the century when a great deal of interest was taken in the famous pirate,
Captain Kidd   He was supposed to
have buried a good deal of treasure
along the Atlantic coast   It was well
understood, however, that it was a dan-
gerous thing to attempt to find this
treasure; for every time the captain
buried one of his iron chests, he killed
one of the pirate crew, and buried his
body with the chest, that the dead man's
ghost might haunt and guard the spot

If you can find the end of a rainbow,

you will be rewarded by also finding a pot of gold at the spot where the rainbow touches the earth.

Don't give to the rich. You will surely come to want if you do.

If you fall up-stairs, that is a sign your credit is rising.

When you see a white horse, put your little finger against your chin just under your lips, and spit over it. The person who does this will find some money soon.

A boy out for a walk will sometimes count all the bows he gets from his friends, and make a cross for each one on a piece of paper that he carries for the purpose. Later he buries the paper. This is supposed to insure his finding as many dollars as he received bows.

DEATH

. .

SNEEZE twice when you first get up, and you will hear of a death before night.

If a dog howls under the window, it foreshadows death in the household.

"There was a dog went and howled under the window of a house up near where I lived. He howled and howled; and they drove him off, but no sooner done it than he was right back again. And in two or three days an old lady that lived there died."

Make your own wedding-dress, and you will not live to wear it out.

When the rain falls in an open grave, it is a sign there will be another death in the same family before the year is out.

Many people are troubled by this saying when the funeral of a friend occurs on a rainy day.

111

To cut the baby's finger-nails before it is a year old will bring it to an early grave. Others say that to cut the baby's finger-nails before its first birthday will make a thief of it

If a whippoorwill sings near the house, it is a sign of death. Some say this is simply a sign of trouble.

A child must not be allowed to look in a mirror before it is a year old, for that means death to it

In "ye olden time" great care was taken of the looking-glass when the family moved, because if it was broken that meant death. Even if the looking-glass was broken in the house and at any time, it was a bad sign. If a picture fell from the wall, that was a very bad omen. There are still those who are "scairt to death" by such accidents.

The sound made by the wood-tick boring in the walls of the old houses was thought to be a forewarning of death. It was known as the "death-watch."

When a loaf of bread in baking splits clear across the top, it means death

A green Christmas makes a full churchyard The foundation for this saying is the fact that open winters

with their constant freezings and thaw-
ings are very unhealthy.

If you go through
a wood or under
a tree in the
e v e n i n g,
and an owl
hoots right
above your
head, it means some
relative or friend of
yours is going to
die within a year.

Thirteen is an un-
lucky number.   If
that number sit down
to eat together, one
of them will die be-
fore the year is out.

If a bird flies in-
to the house, there
will soon be a death
in the family o r
among n e a r rela-
tives.

If a corpse lies over Sunday, there
will be another death in town before the
end of the week. "Never knew that to
fail."

If a dog howls in the yard, the first

person that comes in the door will die very soon. "There was a dog howled in our yard once, and pa was the first one to come in the door. I know ma felt dreadfully about it, and pa died within a year."

Open an umbrella in the house, and you run the risk of bringing on yourself extremely bad luck. If you hold it over your head, it is a sign you are soon to die. If you hold it over another person, you put that person in the same danger.

If a dish breaks when no one is near, it is a warning of death in the family soon.

"When I was a young girl, we had half a dozen slender little wineglasses. They were of thin, clear glass, as pretty as anything you ever see. But they all cracked one after the other as they set there on the mantel with nobody near 'em, and that next summer my mother died."

In the disease called shingles, if the eruption goes way round a person it kills him. Those who recover take a good deal of pride in having it go nearly around.

If you dream of your teeth falling out, that is a sign of death. Even if you dream of the filling falling out that is a bad sign.

A hot May makes a fat graveyard

To have a crow fly over the house is a sign of death.

If three lamps happen to be set on a table at the same time, the result will be that one of the household will die within the year.

Don't let a bat fly into your house If one does get in, kill him, and it will be all right. If the bat gets away, some one of the household will die within a year In the old country, on warm evenings, when they would keep the door open to cool the rooms, you might see a woman standing in the doorway with a broom in her hand to keep the bats out. Every time one flitted past, she would make a fierce whack at it

The child that has long fingers will die young

Others say that long fingers are the sign the child will be an artist or a musician

If a looking-glass gets cracked, it is understood that it is a sign of the death of the eldest son of the household.

The person with a wide cheek will have a long life. The person between whose ear and cheekbone the distance is narrow will die young.

WARTS

. .

HAVE you warts? Rub them all with
a bean, put the bean in an envelope,
and bury it. When the bean sprouts,
the warts will be gone.

To cure a wart, pick it, and let a drop
of blood from it fall on a penny; throw
the penny away, and the person who
picks it up will have the wart.

If you have conscientious scruples
about making other people carry your
warts, you can relieve yourself as follows: Break off a milkweed, rub the
milk on the wart, and bury the milkweed. When it decays, the wart will
disappear. Others say that the juice of
the milkweed will make you have warts.

To cure a wart, rub it with a kernel
of corn Then throw the corn out in
the dooryard, and if a chicken picks it
up and eats it the wart will disappear.

Another way is to steal a piece of
pork to rub the wart with. To do this
so that its use will be effective, you must
visit a neighbor's cellar, and abstract the
meat from his pork-barrel without his
being aware of it

To make your warts go off, rub them
with sassafras

To cure a wart, rub it with a corn,
bore a hole in a tree, put the corn in the
hole, and then plug it in Your wart
will make haste to leave you when you
have done this

Put vinegar on a cent, and let it cor-
rode. Then put the vinegar on your
wart, and the wart will leave

Does that wart still trouble you?
Find a snail, rub the wart with it, and
throw the snail away When the snail
dries up and withers into nothing, the
wart will have gone too.

There are many ways recommended
for getting rid of warts, but very few
ways are suggested by which one can
acquire them One sure method to get
warts is to wash your hands in water
that eggs have been boiled in

If you have a wart you wish to rid yourself of, wait until you see some one riding on a white horse. Then put your finger on the wart, look at the rider and say, " I wish you had my wart — I wish you had my wart." Then he will have it, and you won't.

You can cure your wart if you will steal a dishcloth, rub the wart with it, and then bury the dishcloth.

To get rid of a wart, steal a bean, split it, rub the halves on the wart, and throw them over your shoulder. At the same time say, " Go, wart," and the wart will leave you.

Another way is to do the halves of the bean up, after you have rubbed the wart with them, in a pretty package, and put it in a likely place for some one to pick up. The person who unties the package will have the wart, which at the same time will leave you.

Still another way that is equally good is to sell your warts. A conversation like the following can be held with a friend :

Friend: Do you want to sell your warts ?

Self Yes

Friend. Well, I'll buy them.

Self How much will you give ?

Friend: Five cents.

Self: All right, you can have 'em.

No more need be said, and no money need be paid. The waits know they are fixed when they hear such a conversation, and they make haste to leave.

Handle a toad, and you will have warts

To cure a wart, rub a piece of raw meat on it, and throw the meat into the well, drain, or other place where it will decay quickly. Tell no one; and when the meat has decayed, the wart will have disappeared

A wart can be charmed away in like manner by the use of a bean instead of the meat "I know that's so, because I've tried it myself. The wart went off. I don't care whether any one believes it or not — it's so!"

Some claim it is best, after rubbing your warts with the bean, to write a polite note to the warts, requesting them to go to somebody else, whose name you give Wrap the bean in the note, and throw the whole into the well The warts will presently leave you, and appear on that other person

A certain young man was afflicted with warts Indeed, none of his acquaintance was encumbered to any like degree. One day he told the tale of his warts to a friend who had been a Shaker. This friend had, when in the Shaker community, formed an attachment for a young Shakeress, who had a like fondness for him. Anything beyond a brotherly and sisterly affection was not countenanced among the Shakers, and the two ran away. Now, this young man whose life had been thus romantic told David, his warty friend, that he would cure his warts.

Said he, " How many warts have you? Count them up, and be sure you don't miss any "

David made a careful enumeration, and found fourteen.

" Very well," said the ex-Shaker; " now you go out and find fourteen pebbles, and bring them in."

David brought the pebbles

" Put them in a row," commanded his adviser. " Now take the first, and rub it on one of your warts Remember which one you rub it on. Now you can throw the pebble out of the door, and try the next one "

In this manner he had David rub each wart with one of the pebbles till the last one had been attended to.

" Now," the ex-Shaker concluded, " all
you've got to do is not to think of your
warts for two weeks, and at the end
of that time they will all be gone ; " and
he went his way

David determined to follow the ad-
vice given him, but the harder he tried
not to think of his warts, the more they
were on his mind. At the end of two
weeks, he had still his full quota, and he
felt sure the cure was all a hoax He
thought no more of the matter for a
fortnight or over Then he looked for
his warts, and lo ! they were all gone !

" Did you ever hear of getting rid of
warts by swapping 'em off onto some
one ? That's about as good a way as
there is I had a boy workin' for me
that had over thirty of 'em, and he sold
'em all for a little piece of a pencil not
half an inch long Of course nobody
don't want your warts ; but you keep
stumpin' 'em for a trade, till finally they
make you an offer It don't matter what
it is, even if it ain't more'n a little bit
of a chip — you take the offer, and the
warts 'll leave you and come on that
other fellow I've known ever so many
doin' that "

You can get rid of your warts in this

way. Count them, and tie as many knots in a string as there are warts, and bury the string Dig the string up once a week until the time comes when it has so decayed you cannot find it any more. Then you may be sure your warts will have disappeared.

If you prefer, you can use a stick instead of a string Cut a notch in it for each wart, bury it, and as the stick decays, and the notches disappear, your warts will do likewise.

It is said there used to live a woman in Savoy, Mass , who could "talk a person's warts away."

LOVE AND SENTIMENT

WHEN you go to a wedding, carry away with you a piece of the wedding-cake Sleep with it under your pillow that night, and the person you dream of will be the one you are to marry.

A ring is sometimes put in the wedding-cake. The person who gets the ring will marry within a year.

The person who wishes to know whom he is to marry may settle the question in the following manner Roll up your stockings when you go to bed at night, name them, put them under your pillow, and get into bed over the footboard, backwards If you have a bedfellow, don't speak a word to him after this, and the one of the two girls the stockings were named after that you dream about will be the one you are to marry

Keep track of the white horses you see, and count them up to ninety-nine, and the next person of the opposite sex you shake hands with will be the one you are to marry.

"Why! a girl is sure to marry the first man she shakes hands with after counting ninety-nine white horses, even if he is eighty years old."

The modern girl, particularly if she lives in the city, has it that after counting the requisite number of white horses, she is to note the first person who tips his hat to her. He is her fate.

If three of the same first name sit at table together, one of them will marry within a year.

As long as you keep a piece of wedding-cake in the house, you will have good luck

> Crock mark,
> Sign of a spark.
> Nearer the thumb,
> Sooner he'll come

On Halloween hang up a cabbage-stump over the door. The first person of the opposite sex that comes in is the one you will marry.

Children sometimes try this process to determine whom they like best. Suppose it is a boy who is to make the trial. He gets a companion to name two apple-seeds. Then he takes the apple-seeds, wets them, puts one on the upper lid of each eye, and proceeds to wink as fast as he can.   When one falls off, the companion tells him what girls he named the seeds for, and which was which. The seed which stayed on longest indicates the girl he loves best.

LUCKY DAYS FOR MARRIAGE

Monday for health,
Tuesday for wealth,
Wednesday the best day of all,
Thursday for losses,
Friday for crosses,
And Saturday no day at all.

If the day on which you marry is stormy, it is a sign you are to have a stormy married life.   If it is pleasant, the married life will be pleasant.

On the first night that you sleep in a strange bed, name each of its four posts. If you dream about one of the four persons you named the posts after that person will be the one you will marry.

Unhappily, the person who tries this frequently fails to dream of any one of the four, and, indeed, may not dream at all.

If you sit on a table, it is a sign you will not be married for one year.

Others say that this a sign that you
want to get married

If you braid your hair and accidentally
leave out a little strand, it is a sign you
will be married within a year

A lowery day,
A lowery bride.

This is said with reference to the wed-
ding-day

Never get married until you are able
to cut the nails neatly on both hands

A right-handed person has to acquire
skill by practice to enable him to hold
the knife in his left hand, and cut the
nails on his right nicely.   Apparently
the logic of the saying is that a person
will before acquiring this accomplishment, lack the maturity or capability
which would fit him for such a respon-
sibility   Hence the saying is esteemed
very sensible

If from three lamps set in a row some
person unthinkingly takes one, that is
a sign that person will marry within a
year.

When, of an evening, three persons,
one after another, come into a room and
set a lamp down, it can be accepted as

settled that the third person will marry within the year.

When a person's nose bleeds, it is a sign that the person is lovesick

If by chance you tread on some one's toes. it is a sign that you love that person.

If you are married in a snowstorm, it is a sign that you will be rich

Girls sometimes determine whom they are to marry in this way. On each of twelve slips of paper the girl writes the name of some boy. These she puts in an envelope, and sleeps with them under her pillow. Each morning she draws one of the slips at random, and throws it away. The last one left names the one she is to marry.

When a girl trims pie-crust, and the trimming falls over her hand, it is a sign she is going to marry young.

If, when a young woman tries on a dress in the process of making, it is accidentally pinned to the clothing beneath, that is a sign she will marry soon.

The person who tips a chair over backwards will not marry that year.

May is an unlucky month to marry in.

When three of the same Christian

name meet under the same roof, one of them will marry within the year.

Happy the bride the sun shines on.

The girl who puts on a bridal veil and orange blossoms on any occasion but for her own wedding will never marry

The girl who mops crossways of the boards will marry a drunken husband.

The girl who wets the front of her dress on washing-day will also marry a drunkard.

The girl who in baking scrapes the dough-dish clean will marry a poor man In such a case the wife's thriftiness will tend to keep her husband from remaining poor.

Let a boy light a match, and burn it till a charred end drops. See which way the big end of this points, and that will show where his "best girl" lives.

Light another match, and when one end is charred take hold of that end, and see if you can hold it without breaking till the flame eats clear through to the other end. If you can, it proves that your girl loves you. But if the match breaks in burning, your girl does not care for you.

If a girl can comb and do up her hair

neatly without looking in the glass, it is a sign she won t be an old maid.

Wear a bit of yarrow in your button-hole, if you are anxious to know whom you are to marry. The first person of the opposite sex you meet afterward is your fate

A girl tickles another on the knee and says, —

Tickle, tickle on the knee,
Laugh or smile, an old maid you'll be.

If a laugh or smile results, then both know the tickled one will be an old maid always

When this is tried on a boy, you have to insert the word bachelor in the place of maid in the rhyme

A variation of this theme is the following —

If you're an honest boy (or girl),
As I take you to be,
You'll neither laugh nor smile
While I tickle your knee

If a girl has thirteen after-dinner cof-fee cups given to her within a twelve month, she will be engaged within the year following To bring about this result the one who gave the first one must also present the thirteenth.

Change the name and not the letter,
Change for the worse and not the better.

That is, the girl who marries a man whose last name begins with the same letter as her last name will be worse off than she was before.

When a girl out walking stubs the toe of her right foot, she knows her beau has gone along the same street not long before. If she hurries, she can usually catch up with him.

The boy who dreams of the same girl three nights in succession may know that she is the one he is to marry.

An unhappy life will result if the bride is married in black silk.

The girl who makes a good-looking bed will have a good-looking husband.

If a girl pulls a cabbage, and only a little earth clings to its roots, she is to marry a poor man. If a heavy clod of earth comes up with the cabbage-roots, she will marry a rich man.

Put some apple-seeds on the stove. Get a friend to name them. The one that pops first reveals the person you love best.

WEDDING SIGNS

MARRIED in white, you have chosen all
    right.

Married in gray, you will go far away.

Married in black, you will wish yourself
    back

Married in red, you will wish yourself
    dead

Married in green, ashamed to be seen

Married in blue, he will always be true.

Married in pearl, you will live in a whirl.

Married in yellow, ashamed of your
    fellow.

Married in brown, you will live out of
    town

Married in pink, your fortune will sink.

With a straw or something of the sort
tickle a girl's face or hands. The first
thing she says after the tickling will be
the first thing she will say after she is
married.

The young woman who is fond of cats
will be an old maid.

After a wedding ceremony, it is the
custom for the bride when she leaves
the room, or when she is driving away in
the carriage, to throw back her bouquet
of roses into the midst of the company

The one who gets the bouquet will marry within a year.

If a girl likes cats better than dogs, that is a sign she will never marry.

A girl who finds a crooked pin should hasten to throw it away. If she saves it, she will be an old maid.

If a young man at the supper-table or at a party takes the last biscuit on a plate, he will be an old bachelor. The young woman who does this is likewise fated to live single.

Be careful to sweeten your coffee or tea before you put in the milk. The person who puts in milk first will be crossed in love.

COMPANY

. .

IF you drop the scissors, and they stick up in the floor, it is a sign you are going to have company.

Drop a fork, and if it sticks up in the floor or ground, it is a sign you will have a lady visitor from the direction in which it points. If a knife is dropped and sticks up, a man visitor is coming from the direction in which it points.

"There's no end to these little signs. There's signs for everything."

· When a bumblebee flies in at an open window, look for company soon.

If a visitor leaves any article behind when he goes, it is a sign that he is coming again. Few sayings come true as often as this. The sceptical, however, affirm that natural causes are sufficient to account for the fact.

If the cat in washing its ear rubs its paw way over it, that is a sign of company.

If you knock over the pepper-box.

it is a sign company is coming. The direction it falls in shows the direction the company is coming from.

If you get two pieces of butter on your plate, that is a sign of company.

An itching eyebrow is a sign of company. If the right one itches, the visitor will be a gentleman ; if the left one itches, the visitor will be a lady.

When the palm of the right hand itches, it is a sign of company.

At your home, when you go in at one door and out at another, you may know you are going to have company before the day is out.

You may also know that company is coming when you find the backs of two chairs together.

If you drop a dish-rag, it is well to expect company that day.

If, in sweeping, a bit of charcoal brushed by the broom makes a straight black mark on the floor, it is a sign of company.

In the days of the big wood fires in open fireplaces, it was a very common occurrence for a spark to snap out into the room, and when its fire faded to leave behind a bit of charcoal. This saying had more pertinence then than now.

Sneeze between twelve and one,
Sure sign somebody'll come
Sneeze between one and two,
Come to see you
Sneeze between two and three,
Come to see me.
Sneeze between three and four,
Somebody s at the door

If you have company on Monday, it is a sign you will have company each day through the week.

If the rooster comes up on the step and crows, it is a sign that company is coming

To go up one flight of stairs, and come down another, is a sign that company is coming.

If you make a rhyme unwittingly in your talk, it is a sign company is coming

When a woman forgets to wash the spider, it is a sign that she is going to have company

If you get black on your fingers when making a fire, look out for company

School visitors are coming when a scholar drops his pen, and it sticks up in the floor.

If you go around the chimney, it will bring company

An extra plate at table set,
A hungry guest you soon will get.

Of course the plate must be set by accident, not purposely, or it will bring no guest

You may expect company when you see your cat washing herself. Notice in what direction she faces, for that shows from what direction the company will come.

If your company comes in at one door, and goes out at another, it is a sign of bad luck

Some people are sufficiently affected by this idea that they will be at considerable pains to keep visitors from going out of any door other than the one they came in by.

If you drop your dishcloth, it is a sign that a caller is coming whom you don't want to see.

If you drop the towel, somebody is coming that you do want to see.

RELIGIOUS

· ·

THUNDER, by some, is thought to
be the voice of God. To speak
lightly of it, or jokingly, would be
apt to provoke God's wrath, and
the offender runs the risk of being
punished by getting struck by lightning.

It is supposed that God sometimes punishes people for sin as
soon as it is committed, and with
unmistakable suddenness. Ana-
nias and Sapphira, struck dead for lying,
have many modern counterparts. Sudden death which comes to a bad man,
or a man who has just been swearing
or doing something evil, is by many
thought to be a punishment inflicted
by God. On the other hand, a man
who narrowly escapes death is said to
escape by reason of God's intervention.

Ministers tell such stories as the following: A man was chopping in the
woods. His axe slipped, and gashed his
foot. If the cut had been a quarter-inch

deeper it would have severed an artery, and he would very likely have lost his life. God in his mercy stopped the axe in its course.

Here is another example: A man had prepared to leave this country, and go to Asia as a missionary. He bought his steamer ticket, and was in New York ready to sail. On the morning the boat was to leave he had his coffee served in bed. The waiter was careless, and spilled the hot coffee on the man, so that he was severely scalded. He had to give up his intended journey. He bewailed the accident at the time as a great misfortune, but the ship that he was to have gone in was lost at sea, and all on board perished. The man went later to his chosen field, and did great work for the good cause. God's hand was in the accident that kept him from making that fatal voyage.

When right is apparently worsted, or good men are stricken, with only loss and pain discernible, it is considered a mysterious dispensation of Providence, or it is argued that there is nevertheless some unseen good in what seems on the surface evil.

When a church is struck by lightning,

or is burned, that is supposed to come in the order of nature   But God's wrath is discerned by many when a theatre or saloon is destroyed.   Some said that President Lincoln met his death because he had gone to see a play at a theatre.

In 1848 the first Holyoke dam built across the Connecticut was finished. After the escape of the water had been shut off, and the flood was piling up against the new structure, it is said that the builder exclaimed, "God Almighty couldn t sweep that dam away¹"   The words were no sooner out of his mouth than there was a cracking of timbers, and the whole structure gave way, and crumbled from sight in the torrent of water that then broke loose

People commonly say that the days of miracles ceased nearly two thousand years ago   But in reality most people continue to believe that miracles still frequently occur   Not many think any person has now the power to make a sick man immediately well by laying on of hands, or in any other way   To tell a very sick man to "rise up and walk" with any expectation that he could do so, would be good proof that

you were crazy. Yet it is thought that
God in answer to prayer frequently re-
stores to health those who would natu-
rally die This he rarely, if ever, does
suddenly and at once, as in the days of
old, but gradually, through the ordinary
processes of nature. In 1881, when Gar-
field was shot, a national day of prayer
for his recovery was appointed.

No person is so sick but that God, if
he chooses, can restore health ; but when
a person is dead no one now expects God
to give life back again, or prays for it.
Nor does any one expect if a person
loses a limb that God will make it whole
again. It is not believed that such miracles have ever been done since Bible
times, not but that God could do
them, but he never does, and to ask
that kind of impossibility of him is useless The less likely a thing is to come
about in the usual workings of nature,
the less it is expected that God will in-
terfere and make it come about Rain
is frequently prayed for privately, and
in churches on Sunday, and in extreme
cases, on week days in mass-meetings, of
people that have left business and come
together for the purpose It is not rain
that will come of itself that is expected,

but rain that God will send because it is needed, and is fervently prayed for by many people Something supernatural — a miracle — is hoped for

On such occasions, when the rain comes, it is by many thought that the rain was sent in response to the prayers without which it would have continued dry. There are those who think the people of the present are quite wicked, and bring much evil on themselves by not praying for what they need with the constancy and fervor and trust which characterized our grandparents' prayers

It is a quite common belief that any unnecessary work done on Sunday will bring to grief the project with which it was connected, and that Sunday pursuit of pleasure is very apt to end in mishap.

In some New England families, no one is allowed to read anything but the Bible, the Sunday-school quarterly and Sunday-school books, the *Home Missionary*, and the Boston *Congregationalist*. They expect persons who go outside these lines to come speedily to some bad end

An egg laid on Easter Sunday will never spoil. It will not rot, though it may dry up This is equally true of an egg laid on Good Friday

Wear three new things on Easter, and you will have good luck all that year.

The Baptists in times past used to immerse their converts in the streams The immersing was done entirely independent of weather and seasons. Frequently baptism occurred in midwinter, and a hole had to be cut through the ice for the rite. It was said that in these baptizings no one ever took cold, or was harmed in any other way. In our present days faith has weakened, and the rite is performed in-doors, the converts are clad in suits of waterproof, and the water is warmed

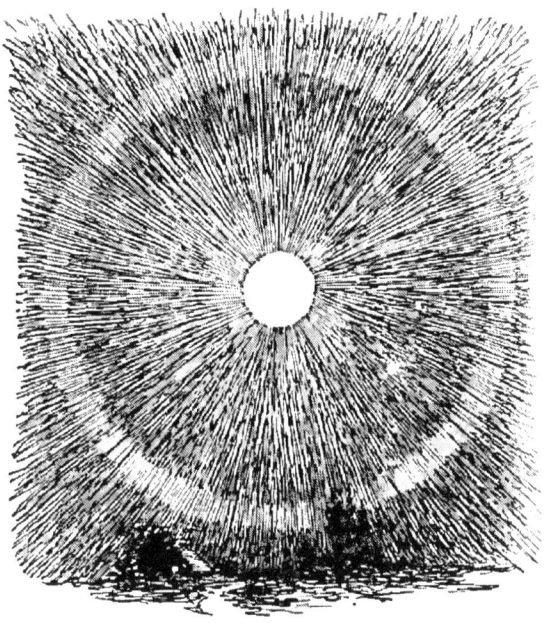

THE MOON

. .

IF there is a circle around the moon, that is a sign it is going to storm. The number of stars you can see within this circle shows how many days distant the storm is. There is some sense in this, in that there would be no circle were the air not hazed with moisture, and the thicker the moisture, of course the fewer the stars that can be seen within the circle — or anywhere else for that matter — and the nearer the storm.

Look at the moon some night and
say, —

" I see the moon, the moon sees me :
The moon sees somebody I want to
see."

Then name the person you wish to
see, and in a day or two you will see
that person

You mustn t sow onions in the new of
the moon They won't amount to much
if you do

Plant corn in the old of the moon
It will ear out better

When you see the new moon, jingle
the money in your pocket, and you will
have money until the next moon comes

What you are doing when you first
see the new moon, you will do much of
while the moon lasts.

When the moon changes, expect a
change of weather

Never expect much of a storm in the
old of the moon

Plant beans in the old of the moon so
that they won't run to vines.

Always set out the slips for your
house-plants in the new of the moon in
August. "They always do so much
better," you will never regret it

Some say that no work prospers unless begun in the new of the moon.

When the new moon appears, observe whether you can hang a powder-horn on its curve or not.   If you can, the month will be a pleasant one   If you cannot, the month will be wet

This, in the days of the fathers, was known as " An old Injun sign."

It was put in words like these   " If the Indian finds he can hang his powder-horn on the new moon, he takes it down, and goes off for a hunt.   If he can't, then he stays at home."   The idea is that the moon is the place whence rains come — that it is a sort of dish which, when sufficiently level, retains the water, but when too much tipped up, allows it to run over the edge.

Wish on the new moon, and you will get whatever you wish for.

Have your hair cut in the new of the moon and it will come out fine and nice.

" When I trim Ben's whiskers and cut his hair in the new of the moon, it grows out as fast again "

The nearer it is to noon when the moon changes, the nearer the next storm is.

But —

> The nearer to midnight,
> The fairer the weather

If, when you first catch sight of the new moon, you see it over your right shoulder, it is a sign of good luck. If the moon is seen over the left shoulder, it is a sign of bad luck. If you see it straight in front of you, it is a sign you are to have a fall. There is a jingle for this last calamity which says, —

> Moon in the face,
> Open disgrace

Kiss the first person you meet after you see the new moon, and you can get whatever you wish for. At any rate, you will at the very least get a present within a month.

Do not kill hogs in the full of the moon. The pork will surely "shrink bilin' in the pot if you do." Neither will you get as much lard when you try the fat.

Kill hogs only in the old of the moon, so that the pork will swell in the spider.

A girl's hair will grow much better if

she is particular to cut it off a little each new moon.

Of the moon's influence on crops, hair-growing, and such things, John Burroughs says: "A second thought must convince one of the absurdity of these notions; since we always have the moon with us, whether we see it or not, and its effect on the earth in causing the tides is just as marked one time as another. If the moon really grew in the sky, and then faded away again, as to the eye alone it appears to do; if the moon was really only the fragment of the sphere, the half-moon only what the eye reports it to be, etc.,—its influence might be much more marked at some times than at others. But we know the full orb passes over us every day, though not always visible. We know the tides are higher when the sun and moon pull together than when they are in opposition, but that these circumstances have any effect on vegetation there is no proof.

"The notion that there is a dry moon and a wet moon is equally erroneous; since it is always dry on some parts of the continent, and always wet in some other parts, or in some other country, and the one moon serves for all. When New England and New York are burning up, the Western or Southern States are usually being drowned out."

When the moon is far north, expect cold weather. When it is far south, expect warm weather.

INSECTS
AND
OTHER
CRITTERS

. .

HANG on to your ears when you sight one of these darning-needles flying around out-doors. If you don't, they will like enough sew up your ears so that you can't hear. If they don't do that, they are liable to make it uncomfortable for you by going right through your head,—in at one ear and out at the other. Besides, they might sting you.

Many New England children are so afraid the darning-needles will do some of these dreadful things that at sight of them they clap their hands over their ears, and run in great terror.

Some say the darning-needles will sew up your mouth or your nose, or they think the creatures will dart straight through your body.

If you kill a toad, and one of your cows catches sight of the dead toad and smells of it, she will give bloody milk

149

This will come true, even if it is one of the children of the household that kills the toad.

It is a common belief among children that angleworms and little toads are rained down. Visible proof of this they find in the fact that these creatures are seen most just after rains. I suppose a heavy rain draws them both out, — the worms come up from their holes and crawl about, and the toads leave the spots where they have buried themselves in the dust the night before, and jump about for some time after the shower is over.

Some say that the worms come out to get a drink, and the toads come out to get the worms.

In case these creatures really are rained down, they ought to be found after showers on city pavements as well as along country roads.

Red lizards are also supposed to be rained down.

If you meet with a lion or a mad bull, or anything of that kind, all you have to do is to look them right in the eye, and they won't touch you. If they do, that proves you did not properly catch the eye of the creature that charged you

If you should ever take a nap out in the fields, sleep with your mouth shut. If you don't, like enough a lizard will crawl in, and go down into your stomach and make trouble there.

It brings bad luck to kill daddy-long-legs and lady-bugs

Don't buy a horse with one white leg. It is a sign of a weak horse.

Give a dog burnt brandy, and it will stunt him so he will stop growing. That's the way these poodles and little terriers are made.

When you buy a horse remember this : --

One white foot try him,
Two white feet buy him,
Three white feet refuse him,
Four white feet and a white nose,
Knock him in the head, and give him to
    the crows.

It is said that a light-colored hoof is softer than a black and has to be shod oftener Light-hoofed horses are therefore not as good as dark The sense of "Two white feet buy him," is explained by the fact that there was a time when a good deal of pride was taken in a horse with white socks or stockings on his hind legs. "Stockings" were white-haired legs up to the knee, while in socks the white stopped lower down.

If a lamb's ears lop over, it is a sign the lamb will die.

It is well for children to remember that if they go out to play on Sunday, the bears will eat them up.

If you don't do what your mother tells you to, the boogers will get you.

The little fellows used to be greatly frightened when they heard a hound baying in the woods; for they understood that a hound dog liked nothing better than to eat up a small boy when he found one handy.

See two white horses, and then the one'll come that you want to go with.

Corner a toad, and it will spit poison at you.

Dogs are said to be healthy animals, and cats unhealthy.

To play with and fondle a cat much will give a person poor health.

The child that plays with a cat that is shedding its hair is liable to get the hair into its stomach and be killed by it.

Many believe that cats will cause the death of babies by sucking their breath. The only reason they suggest for the

action is that the cats are attracted by
the baby's breath because it is sweet.
They will tell you that cats have been
caught in the act, and give much de-
tailed evidence   The story ends with
the killing of the cat, and a great commotion to restore the gasping baby's
breath   Physicians do not credit the
breath-sucking part of the stories, and
I will suggest one or two partial expla-
nations of the phenomena   Firstly, there
might have lingered about the baby's
mouth fragments of a recent lunch that
the cat was removing when found with
its mouth near the baby's ; and secondly, the baby's gasping may have
been caused by fear of the cat, or by
the alarming commotion on its account
among its relatives.

Hold your breath, and you can handle
wasps and bees without fear of being
stung   This recipe has often been tried
with complete success   Some say that
the philosophy of it is that holding the
breath closes the pores of the skin, and
thus makes a person impregnable to the
wasp's sting   I fancy, however, that
the believer insures his safety by hand-
ling the wasps much more surely than
the timid unbeliever would, and does

not give them a chance to use their stingers.

If your cows eat the chestnut blossoms when they fall, it will dry them up.

Others simply say, "The cows dry up when the chestnuts begin to blossom," and affirm that the eating has nothing to do with the matter.

Notice your hens' eggs. The long ones will hatch roosters, and those more nearly round will be pullets.

When you have a tooth pulled, don't leave it lying about. Burn it up. If the cat gets hold of it, the next tooth that comes will be a cat's tooth.

> A swarm of bees in May
> Is worth a load of hay
>
> A swarm of bees in June
> Is worth a silver spoon.
>
> A swarm of bees in July
> Isn't worth a fly.

If the rooster crows in the middle of the night, you may expect soon to hear bad news. It is understood that the direction the rooster's head is pointed indicates whence the bad news will come, and there have been persons who, hearing the rooster's midnight call,

would get up and visit the henroost to
find out in which quarter trouble was
brewing for them

Set a hen on Sunday night, and all the
eggs will hatch   If thirteen eggs are
set, there will hatch from them twelve
pullets and one rooster.

" Eat hog, and you become a hog,"
said one old man to me.   " The only
feller in the world that d gain anything
by it is the shoemaker, because, when he
got turned into a hog, he could reach
around to his back, and pull out a bristle
when he wanted one "

If the breast-bone of the fowl you
have boiled is soft, it was young   If it
is hard, it was old

There is a saying that on the night
before Christmas when the clock strikes
twelve the cows kneel in their stalls.
Some young girls in Hadley, years ago,
sat up to discover whether this was true
or not   At midnight they went out to
the barn, and sure enough when the
hour struck the cows knelt   At any
rate, that was what the girls said.

A still older story told in the town
with the same theme is that at midnight
when the Christmas Day begins, all the
cattle in the yards and fields might be

seen keeeling with their heads turned to
the east in adoration. Two girls of the
olden time, who were eager to see for
themselves whether this was true or not,
sat up on Christmas Eve until the spell-
bound hour, and then visited the farm
cattleyard. But the cattle made no sign
that they were at all affected.

What you are doing when you hear
the first frog in the spring, you will be
doing much of during the year.

If you catch a fish you don't care to
keep, don't throw it back into the water
until you have finished fishing. If you
throw it in before, it will tell all the
other fish what you are up to, and no
more will bite

If you see a white horse, take notice
and in a few moments you will see a
red-headed girl. Even the unbelieving,
if they try it, are astonished at the truth
there is in this statement.

Likewise, if you see a red-headed girl,
take note, and a white horse will soon
come to sight, even if it is not in sight
at the moment.

If your bees swarm, and show signs of
making away, or if a wild swarm flies on
to your premises, you and all your folks
had better " run out and ring bells and

blow horns for all you're worth." The
bees, if not too contrary, will then be
either so charmed or confused that they
will settle down, and all you need do is
to hive them.

Another way to make a swarm of bees
settle is to throw dirt or water at them.
They cannot fly when their wings are
wet. Even the bee that gets drabbled
in the dew has to dry his wings before
he proceeds on his travels.

It is often said that when a bee stings,
it leaves its stinger in the wound, and
that the loss of the stinger later causes
the bee's death. I have at first-hand a
story that tends to disprove this idea.
A man was whetting his scythe when a
bee flew into his face, and stung him on
the tip of his nose. The man dropped
his scythe and whetstone, and grabbed
the bee in his right hand. Before he
could crush the bee, it had stung him
again on his palm. It plainly did not
leave its stinger in the man's nose, else
how could it sting his palm? Both
wounds became equally swollen and
painful.

One old farmer commented on this
statement with regard to the bee in this
way, "Oh, no! a bee doesn't lose his

stinger when he stings half the time.
When he does, and he gets back to the
hive, the old king bee 'll kill him, 'cause
if he ain't got no stinger he can't help
defend 'em any more. If a bee stings
you, and leaves his stinger, you'd better
get it out as quick as you can, or it will
pain you a long time."

The truth of the matter is that a honey
bee does lose its stinger when it stings
a person, and this loss causes its death.
It is different with wasps and bumble-
bees. They will sting a person again
and again with no bad result to themselves. The stings in a series, however, grow less virulent from first to
last.

A rat won't go through a soaped hole.

Ants won't cross a chalk mark. You
simply have to take a piece of chalk, and
draw a circle around the dish you wish
to protect.

In Hadley there was once a dog who
used always to howl when the nine
o'clock evening bell rang. This was
the occasion of not a little talk and
ominous wagging of heads among the
townspeople, who thought it portended
misfortune of some sort.

If you sell a calf, have it taken out

of the barn backwards, and the cow will not mourn its loss so much.

When a horse lies down on the ground to roll, notice whether it rolls over or not. The number of times it rolls over, indicates the number of hundred dollars it is worth.

A cat knows it can go through any hole that it can get its whiskers through without touching. Therefore when a cat comes to a doubtful hole it just puts its head in, and notices whether its whiskers touch or not. If they do, it lets that hole alone.

A girl does well to notice the color of the first butterfly she sees in the spring That will be the color she will wear mostly in her clothes for the next twelve months.

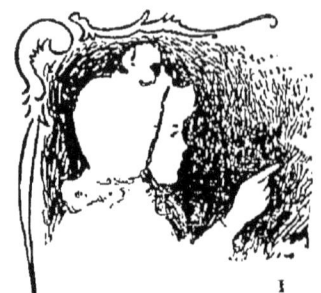

COUNTING
OUT
RHYMES

. .

1

Ene, mene, moni, mi,
Tusca, lona, bona, ski,
Uldy, guldy, boo,
Out go you.

2

Ene, mene, moni, mi,
Barci, loni, boni, stri,
Kay bell, broken well,
We — wo — wack.

3

Ene, mene, moni, mi,
Barca, lona, bona, stri,
Air, wair, from, wack,
Harico, barico, be, bi, bo, buck.

4

Ene, mene, mini, mo,
Catch a nigger by the toe,
When he hollers let him go,
Ene, mene, mini, mo.

5

As I climbed up the apple-tree,
All the apples fell on me.
Did you ever tell a lie?
You did, you know you did.

Because you stole your mother's tea-
    pot lid.

Variation of the foregoing —

As I climbed up the apple-tree,
All the apples fell on me.
Bake a pie, bake a pudden,
Did you ever tell a lie?
Yes, you did, you know you did,
You stole your mother's teapot lid.

6

Red, white, and blue,
All out but you.

7

One, two, three,
Mother caught a flea.
Flea died,
And mother cried,
One, two, three.

8

Eggs, cheese, butter, bread :
Stick, stack, stone dead.
Stick 'em up, stick 'em down,
Stick 'em in the old man's crown.

9

Little boy driving cattle,
Don't you hear his money rattle?
One, two, three, out goes he.
Or she as the case may be.

10

Monkey, monkey, bottle of beer,
How many monkeys have we here?
One, two, three, out goes he
Wire, brier, limber lock,
Six geese in a flock.
Two flew east,
Two flew west,
Two flew over the cuckoo's nest.

11

One, two, three, four, five, six, seven,
All good children go to heaven.

12

My father built a little house,
How many nails did he put in it?

The one pointed out as "it" may say
any number he pleases, but the common
answer is "fifteen." Then those in the
game are counted on, and the one who
is fifteen "is out."

13

A rhyme with the same idea was put
in words like the following —

My father had a horseshoe,
How many nails did he put in it?

The one to whom the last word comes
shuts his eyes, and tries to guess a number which, when the counting begins with

him and goes around, will end with him
That would count him out The guess
has to be made at once ; and if there are
a number in the party, the guess is apt
to be wrong.

In some communities the initial question is as follows : —

> My father has a horse to shoe,
> How many nails do you think'll do?

14

Nigger in the woodpile,
Don't you hear him holler ?
Bring him down to my house,
Give him quarter of a dollar

15

Nigger on the woodpile,
Don't you hear him squeal ?
Bring him down to my house,
Give him a peck of meal.

16

One is all, two is all, zickerzall, zan,
Poptail, vinegar, tickle and tan,
Harum, scarum, English mare-um,
See, taw, buck — uldy, guldy, goo,
Out goes y-o-u.

17

One, two, three, four, five, six, seven,
Count the lovely arch of heaven.

Seven colors make a bow,
Sweetest, fairest thing I know
See the rainbow in the heaven,
One, two, three, four, five, six, seven.

18

One-ery, u-ery, ickery, Ann,
Fillisy, fallasy, Nicholas John,
Quevy, quavy, Irish Mary,
Stinkelum, stankleum, Johnny co
      buck.

A variation of the first two lines runs
as follows : —

Hokey, pokey, winkey, wong,
Chingery, chongery, Nicholas John.

A variation of the third and fourth
lines is this : —

Quevy, quavy, English navy,
Stringelum, strangelum, jolly co
      buck.

19

E-ry, i-ry, ickery Ann,
Bobtail, vinegar, tickle and tan,
Hare-um, scare-um, buckram, bare-
      um,
Tea, tie, toe, tis.

20

The vingle, the vangle,
The goose and the gander,
Come roly me bony brandy dip.

21

Two, four, six, eight,
Mary at the garden gate
Eating cherries off a plate.
Two, four, six, eight

22

As I went up Salt Lake,
I met a little rattlesnake
He e't so much of ginger cake,
It made his little belly ache.

23

Onery, ary, dicory. seven,
Halibone, cralibone, ten or eleven,
Pe, po, must be done,
Twiggle, twaggle, twenty-one.

24

Engine number nine,
Stick your head in turpentine,
Turpentine make it shine,
Engine number nine.

25

Dickery, dickery, dare,
The pig flew up in the air ;
The man in brown
Soon brought him down ;
Dickery, dickery, dare

26

Impty, numpty, tibbity, fig,
Delia, dahlia, dominig,
Ocher, pocher, dominocher,
Om, pom, tuss,
Olly, golly, goo,
Out goes you.

27

Nigger, nigger, hoe potater,
Half past alligatei,
Fiist man killed, a nigger, boo!

28

Ibbity, bibbity, sinity, salve.
Ibbity, bibbity, mellow.

29

Acker, backer, soda cracker,
Acker, backer, boo!
My father chews tobackei,
Out goes you.

30

Monkey in the match-box,
Don't you hear him holler?
Take him to the station-house,
And make him pay a dollai

31

Finally, here is a formula for counting out made up of the first nine letters of the alphabet. The one to whom the letter *I* comes is the one each time who drops out.

A, B, C, D, E, F, G, H, *I*

TRICKS AND CATCHES

Boy Now you say, "Just like me," every time I stop, and I'll tell you a story.

Friend All right.

Boy I went up one flight of stairs.

Friend Just like me.

Boy I went up two flights of stairs.

Friend Just like me.

Boy: I went up three flights of stairs.

Friend. Just like me.

Boy I went up four flights of stairs.

Friend Just like me.

Boy I went into a little room.

Friend Just like me.

Boy. I looked out of a window.

Friend Just like me.

Boy. And I saw a monkey.

Friend Just like me.

Boy Oh, ho, ho, ho! Just like *you!*

The friend collapses, and seeks another boy whom he can try the same on. The boy who knows the catch turns the tables by going through everything right but his final sentence. That he changes

167

to "Just like *you!* Ha, ha, ha! You didn't get me that time!"

There are various rough tricks that have their outbreaks and periods of infliction among school-boys just like measles or whooping-cough. One of these is the making another fellow "walk Spanish." You catch him by the collar and the slack of his pants behind, and make him step along on the tips of his toes. The walker feels very awkward and helpless, and the other fellows are very much amused by his manner. This performance is also called "The Shirt-tail Run."

"The Dutch Whirl" is considered a very clever thing among the boys. Two of them catch a third between them, each with a grip on his coatsleeve and "pant-leg," and turn him over and land him on his feet again. It makes the whirled one a little dizzy and disconcerted, but has no serious effect if his clothing holds.

Say the following over and over as fast as you can —

1. Six gray geese in a green field grazing

2. Six, slick, slim saplings.

3. Theophilus Thistledown, the suc-

cessful thistle sifter, in sifting a sieve full of unsifted thistles, thrust three thousand thistles through the thick of his thumb   If, then, Theophilus Thistledown, the successful thistle sifter, in sifting a sieve full of unsifted thistles, thrust three thousand thistles through the thick of his thumb, see that thou, in sifting a sieve full of unsifted thistles, dost not get the thistles stuck in thy tongue.

4 Six, thick, thistle sticks

5   A cup of coffee in a copper coffee-pot

6. The cat ran up the ladder with a raw lump of liver in its mouth

This is likewise repeated in this form   —

The cat ran over the roof of the house with a lump of raw liver in her mouth.

7   Round and round the rugged rock the ragged rascal ran

A boy asks a friend to play a number game with him   After he has given the friend the necessary rudimentary instruction, the game proceeds in the following dialogue   —

Boy · I one it.
Friend   I two it.
Boy   I three it.
Friend · I four it.
Boy.   I five it.
Friend   I six it.
Boy : I seven it.
Friend.   I eight it.

Boy · Oh, you *ate* the old dead horse ! (or some other subject equally choice for eating purposes).

If the friend knows the trick, he, at the end, changes the final sentence to " *You* ate it."

ANCIENT JOKE

First person   Did you ever notice that when you get up in the morning it is always your left foot that you dress last ?

Second person   No, and I don't believe it is, either.

First person   Well, whichever foot you dress first, the other must be the *left* one, mustn't it ?

When this point has been made, it is proper that the company should laugh.

A CHICKEN QUESTION

Boy to companion   Which would you rather have, a rooster or a pullet ?

If boy number two says "a rooster,"
boy number one goes behind him, and
gives him a hoist with his knee.

Is he says " a pullet," number one
pulls number two's nose.

Number one considers himself very
smart in either case

A PRESENT

Boy Don't you want me to give you
a little red box?

Companion Yes.

The boy then gives the other a box
on the ear

THE ARREST

Boy number one You're going to be
'rested.

Boy number two When?

Boy number one When you go to bed
to-night

A MOTHER'S CALL

Boy to companion Your mother calls
you Harry (or whatever the other fellow's name is)

Harry What for?

Boy: Because that's your name

A SERIOUS CHARGE

Boy You're going to be arrested.

Friend What for?

Boy · For stealin your grandpa's toe-nails.

INNUENDO

When two boys in school go for a drink to the waterpail at the same time, number one hands the glass to number two and says, " Age before beauty." Number two takes it, and says, " Men before monkeys." Number one finishes the dialogue and keeps up his end by responding, "The dirt before the broom."

THE MONKEY AT SCHOOL

First child. Do you want to see a monkey?

Second child Yes.

Then number one holds up a mirror before number two, or goes outside and holds a dark shawl up against the window-pane for number two to look into

A FOREIGN LANGUAGE

Hog Latin " Igry knowgry somegry thinggry yougry don'tgry knowgry."

Translation " I know something you don't know."

A conversation carried on in this language between two children is as blind to their uninitiated mates as real Latin.

How the speakers can make anything
out of such outlandish grunting talk is a
great puzzle. But children find it even
more difficult than grown people to keep
a secret, and this accomplishment is not
long in becoming a common possession.

RHYMES AND JINGLES

. .

WHEN about to run a race or
engage in a jumping-match, this
rhyme is appropriate : —

> One to begin,
> Two to show,
> Three to make ready,
> And four to go.

At the end of the race the one
who came in last sometimes con-
soles himself by calling out : —

> First's the worst,
> Second's the same,
> Last's the best of all the game.

Question : What's your name ?
Answer : Pudden tame ;
> Ask me again
> And I'll tell you the same.

Some of the boys give a much ruder
answer to this question in these words : —

John Brown,
Ask me again and I'll knock you down.

Second form —

Question What's your name?
Answer Pudden tame
Question What's your natur'?
Answer Pudden tater
Question What's your will?
Answer. Pudden swill.

Third form —

Question What's your name?
Answer. Pudden tame.
Question What's your other?
Answer Bread and butter.
Question Where do you live?
Answer In a sieve
Question What's your number?
Answer Cucumber

Crowing hens and jumping sheep
Are the worst property a farmer can
     keep.

Boys often say it in this way —

   Whistling girls and crowing hens
   Always come to some bad ends

Another version is —

Whistling girls and blatting sheep
Are the worst property a farmer can
     keep

Still another way to say the same thing is : —

Whistling girls and hens that crow
Are always sure to get a blow.

The girl's response to this innuendo is, " That is not right   It's like this : —

Whistling girls and merino sheep
Are the *best* property a farmer can keep."

When a boy gets mad at another he will sometimes call out derisively : —

Paddy Whacker, chew tobacker,
If he dies, it is no matter.

In the following, two children stand and take hold of hands, and swing their arms from side to side in time to the rhythm of the verse they repeat   With the final words, hands still clasped, they turn the arms on one side over their heads and at the same time turn around themselves   The verse runs as follows —

Wash your mother's dishes,
Hang 'em on the bushes.
When the bushes begin to crack,
Hang 'em on the nigger's back
When the nigger begins to run,
Shoot him with a leather gun

The following is a programme for Thanksgiving week : —

>Monday — wash,
>Tuesday — scour,
>Wednesday — bake,
>Thursday — devour

In a game of tag, it is the proper thing to shout out to the one in chase —

>Fire on the mountain,
>Fire on the sea,
>You can't catch me

A variation : —

>Fire on the mountain,
>Run, boys, run ;
>The cat's in the cream-pot,
>Run, girls, run !

A quick way of counting up to one hundred : —

Ten, ten, double ten, forty-five, fifteen

William Blake, William Austin, and William Bond all lived in the same town This fact inspired some local poet with the following strains, that proved quite popular among the young people : —

Bill Blake made the cake,
Bill Austin made the frostin,
And Bill Bond put it on.

Rhyme addressed to a person who
has red hair : —

Redny, redny, fire on top,
All the rednys come flipperty flop.

When you are getting ready to jump,
swing your arms and say this : —

One, two, three,
The bumble bee,
The rooster crows,
And away he goes.

Lazy folks work the best
When the sun is in the west.

This rhyme the women folks like to
repeat to the men folks when the latter
find it necessary to work in the evening.

A suitable address to a Frenchman is
the following : —

Frenchy baboo
Lived in a shoe,
Never got up till half-past two.

A French citizen can respond to the
American in terms like these : —

Yankee Doodle went to town,
Stuck a feather in his crown,
Called him Macaroni

Another derisive rhyme employed
against the French is this : —

Pea-soup and Johnny-cake
Make a Frenchman's belly ache

There was a little man,
He had a little gun,
He put it in his pocket,
And away he did run.

Variation : —

There was a little man,
He had a little gun,
His bullets were made of lead,
And he went out to shoot the duck,
And shot him right in the head.
Then away he did run to old Granny
    Jones
Because there was a fire to make,
Saying, "Here is the duck I shot in the
    brook,
And now I'll go after the drake."

Little Dick,
He was so quick,
He tumbled over the timber,

He bent his bow,
To shoot a crow,
And shot the cat in the winder

If a body meet a body in a bag of beans,
Can a body tell a body what a body
means ?

A MODERN MOTHER GOOSE

THE hero of this tale was probably
very like many of the makers of the
chance jingles that have caught the
children's ears, and become immortal
by much repetition

He is said to have lived in Enfield,
Conn.   One morning, in schooltime, he
wrote something on a slip of paper and
passed it round among his fellows   It
made a good deal of ill-concealed mer-
riment, and the teacher was fortunate
enough to capture the offending bit of
paper and to ferret out its author   The
words on the paper were, —

Three little mice ran up the stairs
To hear Miss Blodgett say her prayers

The teacher realized that she was
being made fun of, but was so impressed
by the clever expression of the lines that
she said, " John, I give you five minutes

to make another two lines.   If you fail,
I shall punish you."

The boy scratched his head, and went
to work.   The result was as follows : —

When Miss Blodgett said " Amen,"
The three little mice ran down again.

One person says to another · —

Adam and Eve and Pinchme
Went out for a swim ,
Adam and Eve got drowned,
Who was saved ?

The second person answers, " Pinchme."

Number one responds by giving number two a pinch.

Old rhyme : —

Said Aaron to Moses,
" Let's cut off our noses·
Says Moses to Aaron,
" It's the fashion to wear 'em."

Indian counting up to twenty : —

Een, teen, tether, fether, fip,
Satra, latra, co, tethery, dick,
Eendick, teendick, tetherdick, fether-
    dick, bump,

Eenbump, teenbump, tetherbump, feth-
erbump, jicket

A boy ties another's stockings together, and then hollers as loud as he
can, —
> " Charlo beef,
> The beef was tough,
> Poor little Charley
> Couldn t get enough "

The name in the third line is changed
to suit the case in hand
This stocking-tying is usually done
by a boy's friends while he is in swim-
ming, and the jokers try to tie such a
knot that the owner can only untie it by
using his teeth   The appropriate time
to say the poetry is when the boy begins to work with his teeth on the knot.
Here is a variation —

> Chew, chew — the beef.
> The beef is tough,
> If you don't chew hard,
> You'll never get enough.

If a boy has a friend named Joseph,
he can entertain him by the following
rhyme —

> Joe, Joe,
> Broke his toe
> Riding on a buffalo

If the friend's name is Frank. the following will suit : —

> Frank. Frank,
> Turned the crank,
> His mother come out and gave him
>   a spank,
> And knocked him over the sand-
>   bank.

If his name is Bert the following is appropriate · —

> Bert, Bert, tore his shirt
> Riding on a lump of dirt.

If his name is Samuel, he will very likely be interested in this · —

Sam, Sam,
The dirty man,
Washed his face in a frying-pan,
Combed his hair with the back of a
    chair.
And danced with the toothache in the
    air.

Something like the above ditty is appropriate for a boy named John. The accepted way to repeat the jingle is as follows . —

> My son John is a nice old man,
> Washed his face in a frying-pan,

Combed his hair with a wagon-wheel,
And died with the toothache in his
heel.

Take the baby's foot in your hand,
wiggle the toes one after the other, beginning with the big one, and recite : —

This little pig says, " I go steal wheat , "
This little pig says, " Where'll you get
it ? "
This little pig says, " In father's barn , "
This little pig says, " I go tell , "
And this little pig says, " Quee, quee,
quee ! "

A variation of this story is the following : —

This little pig goes to market,
This little pig stays at home,
This little pig has plenty to eat,
This little pig has none.
This little pig says, " Wee, wee, wee ! "
all the way home.

One of close resemblance to the above
is this : —

This little pig says, " I want some corn ; "
This little pig says, " Where'll you get
it ? "
This little pig says, " In grandpa's barn, "

This little pig says, " It'll do no harm, "
This little pig says, " Quee, quee, quee,
   I can't get over the barn door-sill ! "

Another toe refrain is the following,
which begins with the smallest of the
five : —

> Little Pee,
> Penny Rue,
> Ludy Whistle,
> Mary Hustle,
> Great big Tom, gobble, gobble !

A burlesque —

> The boy stood on the burning deck,
> Peeling potatoes by the peck
> When all but he had fled,   .
> He cried aloud and said,
> " Say ! father, say !
> Shall I throw the peels away ? "

Second form : —

> The boy stood on the burning deck,
> Eating peanuts by the peck.
> His father called , he could not go,
> Because he did love peanuts so

Third form · —

> The boy stood on the burning deck,
> Eating peanuts by the peck.

A girl stood by all dressed in blue,
And said, "I guess I'll have some too."

A verse for a small boy : —

Fishy, fishy, in the brook,
Papa catch him with a hook,
Mama fry him in a pan,
Georgy eat him fast's he can.

The last line sometimes ends, "like a man"

The last two lines may also be changed to read : —

Mama fry him in the spider,
Georgy eat him like a tiger.

The boy's name can be varied to suit the speaker.

One way of counting to ten : —

Onery, twoery, fithery, sithery, san,
Wheelerbone, whackerbone, inery,
ninery, tan.

A verse said by a boy who parts from his companion in the evening : —

Good-night,
Sleep tight,
Don't let the bedbugs bite.

A political couplet shouted by school-boys : —

Republican rats, take off your hats,
And make way for the Democrats

A jingle to say when churning : —

> Come, butter, come,
> Peter's at the gate,
> Waiting for a patty cake.

This used to be said as a charm to
make the butter come quickly.

The schoolhouse at the little Massachusetts village of Hockanum seventy-
five years ago was far too small to
accommodate the outpouring of the
population on the momentous occasion
of a "last day," and it was the custom
to have the exercises in the long hall of
" Granther " Lyman's tavern   The piece
which created the greatest sensation on
one of these last days was delivered before a crowded audience by a certain
small boy in the following words : —

A woodchuck lived far over the hills, a
     good way off,
And died with the whooping-cough

It bears every mark of being original
poetry, and it was repeated and laughed
over for a long time afterwards

Whether this boy originated the idea

and expression or not, there are at the present time extended variations of the tale. The best of these is the following : —

Over the hills and a good way off,
A woodchuck died with the whooping-
cough.
The thunders rolled, the lightnings
flashed,
And broke grandma's teapot all to
smash — down cellar.

When you have the baby in your lap, you can amuse it by saying, —

"Pat a cake, pat a cake, baker's man."
"So I will, master, as fast as I can."
"Roll it, roll it, roll it,
Prick it, prick it, prick it,
Toss it up in the oven and bake it."

You at the same time take the baby's hands in yours, and pat them together to suit the two first lines, rub them against each other to suit the third, take one finger and dig it into the palm of the other hand to suit the fourth, and toss both hands up, and the baby too if you choose, to suit the final line. Then, if the baby is anything like the babies

used to be, it will crow and be very
happy.

Here is a variation of the same
theme · —

Pat a cake, pat a cake, baker's man,
Pat it and pat it as fast as you can,
Pat it and prick it, and mark it with B,
And toss it in the oven for baby and me.

This is acted out in the same way,
and the letter B is marked with a finger
on the child's palm   B, of course, stands
for baby.

Jog the baby up and down on your
knees, and say, —

> Trot, trot to Boston,
> To buy a loaf of bread
> Trot, trot home again,
> The old trot's dead

Trot the baby on your knee, and say. —

Seesaw, Jack in the hedge,
Which is the way to London Bridge?

When you have the baby in your
arms and are rocking it to sleep, say, —

> Bye baby bunting,
> Papa's gone a-hunting ;

Mother's gone to milk the cow,
Sister's gone — *I* don't know how,
Brother's gone to get a skin
To wrap the baby bunting in

Whether it is a nurse or one of the sisters of the infant that is supposed to say this is not quite clear.

Catch a grasshopper, and say to it, —

Grasshopper, grasshopper, give me some
    molasses,
Or I'll kill you to-day, and bury you to-
    morrow

When you are asked to tell a story, or to furnish amusement of most any sort, you can say, —

I'll tell you a story
About old Mother Morey,
And now my story's begun,
I'll tell you another
About her brother,
And now my story is done

Or you can put it in this form : —

I'll tell you a story
About Jack a Nory;
And he had a calf,
And that's half,

And he threw it over the wall,
And that's all.

Two children sit opposite each other
with their palms on their knees. They
say this rhyme together, and clap each
other's hands in time to the metre : —

Bean porridge hot,
Bean porridge cold,
Bean porridge's best
When nine days old.

In the English version, it is pease porridge or pease pudding, but New Englanders are not acquainted with those
dishes

The child's hands in the following are
put palm down on the table. Go over
the fingers one word to each to the end
of the incantation. The finger that has
the final word is turned under. Go over
the remaining nine with the same lingo,
and turn under the one that comes last.
Repeat the process till all are turned
under.

Intra, mintra, cute-ra corn,
Apple-seed and apple-thorn,
Wire, brier, limber lock,
Six geese in a flock.

Sit and sing by the spring,
O-u-t, out, up on yonder hill
There sits old Father Wells,
He has jewels, he has rings,
He has many pretty things,
Whip-jack, two nails, blow the bel-
    lows out, old man

This is also said as follows —

Intra, mintra, cute-ra, corn,
Apple-seed, and apple-thorn,
Wire, brier, limber lock,
Six geese in a flock,
Seven sit by the spring,
O-u-t, out,
Hang mother s dishcloth out,
Fling, flang, flash it off

THE WEEK

Wash on Monday,
Iron on Tuesday,
Bake on Wednesday,
Brew on Thursday,
Churn on Friday,
Mend on Saturday,
Go to meeting on Sunday

A girl will sometimes make the following remarks to the new moon I have
never heard that the revelation was made

to her that she prayed for — at any rate,
not by the moon.

New moon, new moon, pray tell to me
Who my true love is to be —
The color of his hair,
The clothes he will wear,
And the day he'll be wedded to me

If before April first one boy tries to
fool another, boy number two squelches
the would-be fooler by saying, —

April fool's a-coming,
And you're the biggest fool a-run-
ning.

If the attempt is made after April first,
he says. —

April fool is past.
And you're the biggest fool at last

A rhyme that does service for both
occasions is this —

Up the ladder, and down the tree,
You're a bigger fool than me.

A JINGLE FOR THE BABY'S FEET

Shoe the old horse, shoe the old mare,
Drive a nail here, and drive a nail there;
But let the little nobby colt go bare.

When you say, " Shoe the old horse," pat the bottom of the baby's right foot to imitate the driving of nails When you say, " Shoe the old mare," pat the left foot Continue this process in the second line, first the right foot, then the left   In the final line it is imagined that the little nobby colt kicks up its heels, and you must catch the baby's ankles, and give them a grand toss to suit this idea

Boy number one inquires of boy number two, " What do you do when your mother licks you ? "

Boy number two replies, —

" Ice-cream
Made by steam,
Sold by a donkey in a charcoal team "

At picnics you will sometimes hear the children say, —

Lemonade,
Made in the shade,
Stirred with a spade,
By an old maid

The children at one time used to enjoy shouting at each other the following poem —

Oh, what is the use
Of chewing tobacco,
And spitting the juice?

Whether it was the rhythm and rhyme of the piece or its moral sentiment that was so pleasing to them is uncertain.

Here is one way to amuse a child Clasp your hands with the fingers turned inward, and repeat the following ditty, which you illustrate by changing the position of your fingers and hands : —

Here's a meeting-house, there's the
    steeple,
Look inside and see all the people.
Here's the singers going up-stairs,
And here's the minister saying his
    prayers.

To make the steeple, elevate your forefingers with the tips joined. To suit the second line open your hands a little, and wiggle the ends of your clasped fingers. Illustrate the singers going up-stairs by making the fingers of your right hand walk up those of your left. Lastly, clinch your hands, put one fist on top of the other, and that is the minister.

When a schoolboy wishes to be humorous, he will sometimes call out to a companion, —

"Can you read, can you write,
Can you smoke your daddy's pipe?"

A small girl who wishes her companions to understand that she is overcome by ennui will sometimes sighingly remark, —

"Oh, dear, bread and beer,
If I was home I shouldn't be here!"

A FINGER POEM

Five little rabbits went out to walk,
They liked to boast as well as talk.
The first one said, " I hear a gun!"
The second one said, " I will not run!"
Two little ones said, "Let's sit in the
    shade;"
The big one said, "I'm not afraid!"
Bang, bang! went a gun,
And the five little rabbits run.

The child holds up one of its hands while it repeats these lines. The fingers are the five rabbits. With his other hand he takes hold of each finger in turn as he speaks of the rabbit it represents. "The first one" is the thumb. "The second one" is the forefinger.

" The two little ones " are the two final
fingers. " The big one " is the middle
finger.

A SCHOOLBOY JINGLE

" Fire, fire ! "
Said Mrs. McGuire.
" Where, where ? "
Said Mrs Ware.
" Down town ! "
Said Mrs Brown.
" Oh, Lord save us ! "
Said Mrs. Davis.

ANOTHER JINGLE

Two's a couple,
Three's a crowd,
Four on the sidewalk
Is never allowed.

NURSERY TALES

THE OLD WOMAN AND HER PIG

ONCE there was an old woman found a sixpence while she was sweeping. and she took it to the village and bought a little pig with it.

She got part way home. and she came to a stile, and the pig wouldn't go over the stile.

So she told her little dog to bite the pig, and he wouldn't.

Then she went along a little way, and she came to a stick that was lying by the side of the road. And she said, "Stick, stick, beat dog, dog won't bite pig, piggy won't jump over the stile; I see by the moonlight 'tis half-past midnight, time pig and I were home an hour and a half ago."

But the stick wouldn't.

Then she went along a little way, and

she came to a fire that was burning by
the side of the road   And she said, " Fire,
fire, burn stick, stick won't beat dog, dog
won't bite pig, piggy won't jump over the
stile ; I see by the moonlight 'tis half-
past midnight, time pig and I were home
an hour and a half ago.

But the fire wouldn't.

Then she went along a little way,
and she came to a puddle of water in
the road.   And she said, " Water, water,
quench fire, fire won't burn stick, stick
won't beat dog, dog won't bite pig,
piggy won't jump over the stile , I see
by the moonlight 'tis half-past midnight, time pig and I were home an
hour and a half ago."

But the water wouldn't

Then she went along a little way,
and she saw an ox standing in a field.
And she said, " Ox, ox, drink water,
water won't quench fire, fire won't burn
stick, stick won't beat dog, dog won't
bite pig, piggy won't jump over the
stile , I see by the moonlight 'tis half-
past midnight, time pig and I were home
an hour and a half ago "

But the ox wouldn't.

Then she went along a little way,
and she came to a butcher standing in

the door of his shop. And she said,
"Butcher, butcher, kill ox, ox won't
drink water, water won t quench fire,
fire won't burn stick, stick won't beat
dog, dog won't bite pig. piggy won't
jump over the stile ; I see by the moonlight 'tis half-past midnight, time pig and
I were home an hour and a half ago "

But the butcher wouldn t

Then she went along a little way,
and she saw a rope tied to the limb
of a tree And she said, " Rope, rope,
hang butcher, butcher won't kill ox, ox
won't drink water, water won't quench
fire. fire won't burn stick, stick won't
beat dog, dog won't bite pig. piggy won't
jump over the stile , I see by the moonlight 'tis half-past midnight, time pig and
I were home an hour and a half ago."

But the rope wouldn't.

Then she went along a little way,
and she saw a rat. And she said, " Rat,
rat, gnaw rope, rope won't hang butcher,
butcher won't kill ox, ox won't drink
water, water won't quench fire, fire won't
burn stick, stick won't beat dog, dog
won't bite pig, piggy won t jump over
the stile , I see by the moonlight, 'tis
half-past midnight, time pig and I were
home an hour and a half ago "

But the rat wouldn't

And the little old woman said to the rat, " I'll cut off your tail, then."

So the rat began to gnaw the rope, and the rope began to hang the butcher, and the butcher began to kill the ox, and the ox began to drink the water, and the water began to quench the fire, and the fire began to burn the stick, and the stick began to beat the dog, and the dog began to bite the pig, and the pig began to jump over the stile, and the little old woman got home that night.

This story has a number of variations, and in the following paragraphs is given a fragment of one of them : —

" As I was passing over London bridge I found a kid.   And I said, ' Kid, kid, jump over the moon '

" Kid wouldn't jump over the moon. 'Tis past midnight; time kid and I were home an hour and a half ago

"Then I went along a little farther, and I came to a dog.   And I said, ' Dog dog, bite kid ; kid won't jump over the moon.   'Tis past midnight, time kid and I were home an hour and a half ago.' '

It was an old farmer over ninety years old who was husking corn in a hillside field that tried to repeat this to me.   I told him I did not see what the woman wanted the kid to go over the moon for. "I don't see any sense in that," I said.

"Well," was the response, "what's the sense of any of it? All these things you're gettin' are just like that. There ain't no sense in any on 'em."

I was not convinced, but I could think of no satisfactory answer.

The following is probably a more correct version of what this old farmer tried to repeat : —

"As I went over London Bridge I lost a guinea and found a kid, and the kid wouldn't go. See, by the moonlight, 'tis half-past midnight — time kid and I were home an hour and a half ago.

"Then I went along a little way, and I found a staff, and I said, ' Pray, staff, lick kid ; kid won't go,' " etc.

In still another telling, the old woman, instead of remarking the lateness of the hour by the moon, says, " Piggy won't jump over the stile, and I sha'n't get home in time to get my old man's supper to-night.'

THE FOX AND THE LITTLE RED HEN.

Once upon a time there was a little red hen lived in the edge of some woods.

On the other side of the woods lived
an old fox with his mother.

One day the old fox said to his
mother, " Now, mother, you have the
pot boiling, I'm going to catch the little
red hen, and we'll have her for dinner."

So he slung a bag over his shoulder,
and started for the little red hen's house

The little red hen was out in the yard
picking up chips to make a fire to boil
her teakettle with So the old fox
slipped into the house, and hid behind
the door

Pretty soon the little red hen came in
with her apron full of chips She turned
around to lock the door, and she saw the
old fox Then she was so frightened
that she dropped all her chips, and flew
up to a peg in the wall.

The old fox laughed and said, " Ha,
ha! I'll soon bring you down off from
there."

Then he began running round and
round after his tail

The little red hen kept turning around
on the peg to watch him, and she got so
dizzy after a little that she fell off

Then the old fox picked her up, and
put her in his bag, and started home
feeling very fine.

By and by the little red hen began to wonder if she could get out. She didn't want to be eaten for dinner that night, and she happened to think she had her scissors in her pocket. So she took them out, and snipped a hole in the bag and jumped out.

Then she picked up some stones in the road, and put them in the bag in her place, and ran home as fast as she could go.

By and by the old fox said to himself, " How heavy this little red hen is. She's so plump and fat, won't she make a good dinner!" and he smacked his lips to think of it.

When he came in sight of the house his mother stood in the door watching for him, and he called out, " Hi, mother, have you got the pot boiling?"

His mother said, " Yes, yes, have you got the little red hen?"

And he answered, " Yes; and she'll make a fine dinner. Now, when I say three, you take the cover off, and I'll pop her in."

" All right," says his mother.

" All ready," says the fox, " one, two, three."

His mother took the cover off, and

plump went the stones into the boiling water, and the pot tipped over and scalded the old fox and his mother to death.

But the little red hen lives in the woods by herself yet.

JACK AND THE BEANSTALK

One day there was a woman sweeping her floor, and she swept up a little bean. She didn't know nothing where it came from, and she swept it along and along, and might 'a' swept it into the fireplace, but her little boy saw it, and he picked it up, and said, "I'm goin' to plant this bean, mother."

He took it out in the garden, and dug a hole and planted it. After that he was all the time runnin' out to see if his bean had come up, and when it did come up he was all the time runnin' out to see how it was growin'.

It didn't take it but a day to get as high as the window-sill. Next day it was as high as the house. Next day after that it was as high as the meetin'-house steeple. So it kept growin' until it got so high the top hitched on to one of the horns of the moon.

Then the little boy said he was goin'

to climb it. He climbed up till he got
to the moon, and when he got there he
went along till he came to an old giant's
house up there.

That night he crep' into the house,
and got in where the giant was sleep-
in'. The bed was covered with a great
nice quilt, and Jack thought he'd have
it. All along the edge was lots of little
bells that went tinkle, tinkle, when he
began to pull it

The giant heard him and called out,
"Who's round my house this dark, bloody
night?"

Jack didn't say nothin', and when all
was quiet he pulled the bedquilt off a
little farther. The bells went tinkle,
tinkle, and the giant woke up and called
out, "Who's round my house this dark,
bloody night?"

Jack kept still, and every time the
giant fell asleep he pulled off a little
more of the bedquilt, till finally he had
it all, and ran away. He got to the
beanstalk, and called out, "Hump it
and bump it, and down I go"

Then he slid down, and carried the
bedquilt in to his mother.

After a while the little boy thought
he'd go up again, and he brought away

something more of the giant's. He
kept on that way goin' up every few
days till I s'pose he got pretty much
all that the old giant up there in the
moon owned

But there was one time the old giant
caught Jack at it, and he put after him.
Jack was a good runner, and he got to
the beanstalk first, and he called out,
"Hump it and bump it, and down I
go."

He slid down so fast that he got to
the ground before the giant was half-
way down. Then he took his hatchet
and chopped off the beanstalk, and the
giant came tumbling down and was
killed.

After that Jack and his mother were
rich people.

THE LITTLE MOUSE WITH THE LONG TAIL.

The children in old times thought
this one of the best stories that ever
was. The oven spoken of was the brick
opening at the side of the old kitchen
fireplace where baking was done. When
not in use it was a very comfortable
place for the cat to jump up to and nap
in The mouse could come down the

flue that connected the oven with the chimney, or in at some crevice.

Once there was an old cat in the oven spinin' and spinin'.

Bimeby there came along a little mouse, and the old cat bit its tail off

Then the little mouse said, "Pray, cat, give me my great long tail again"

And the old cat said, "Well, go to the cow and get me some milk."

So first he hopped and then he jumped, and quickly he came to a good old cow again.

Then the mouse said, "Pray, cow, give me milk, I give cat milk, cat give me my great long tail again"

And the old cow said, "Well, go to the barn and get me some hay"

So first he hopped and then he jumped, and quickly he came to a good old barn again.

Then the mouse said, "Pray, barn, give me hay, cow give me milk, cat give me my great long tail again."

And the barn said, "Well, go to the smith and get me the key"

So first he hopped and then he jumped, and quickly he came to a good old smith again.

Then the mouse said, "Pray, smith,

give me key, barn give me hay, cow give me milk, cat give me my great long tail again."

And the smith said, "Well, go to the coaler, and get me some coal."

So first he hopped, and then he jumped, and quickly he came to the good old coaler again.

Then the mouse said, "Pray, coaler, give me coal, smith give me key, barn give me hay, cow give me milk, cat give me my great long tail again."

So the coaler gave him the coal, and the smith gave him the key, and the barn gave him hay, and the cow gave him milk, and the little mouse gave the milk to the cat, and got his great long tail again.

The teller of the story made every repetition of the word ' tail ' long drawn out and emphatic.

In a variation of this story the mouse is sent by the cow to the men at work in the meadow for the hay. The men send the mouse to the brook for water, but finally, after various trials and tribulations, the mouse gets his great long tail again.

At the beginning of the story, where it speaks of the cat spinning, it means that she was purring

THE LITTLE RED HEN AND THE WHEAT

Once there was a little red hen found a grain of wheat in the barnyard, and she said, "Who will plant this wheat?"

"I won't," says the dog.

"I won't," says the cat.

"I won't," says the goose.

"I won't," says the turkey.

"I will, then," says the little red hen.

So she planted the grain of wheat. After a while the wheat grew up and was ripe.

"Who will reap this wheat?" says the little red hen.

"I won't," says the dog.

"I won't," says the cat.

"I won't," says the goose.

"I won't," says the turkey.

"I will, then," says the little red hen. So she harvested the wheat.

"Who will thrash this wheat?" says the little red hen.

"I won't," says the dog.

"I won't," says the cat.

"I won't," says the goose.

"I won't," says the turkey.

"I will, then," says the little red hen. So she thrashed the wheat.

"Who will take this wheat to mill to

have it ground?" says the little red hen

"I won t," says the dog

"I won't," says the cat.

"I won't," says the goose.

"I won't," says the turkey

"I will, then," says the little red hen So she took the wheat to mill, and by and by she came back with the flour.

"Who will bake this flour?" says the little red hen

"I won't," says the dog.

"I won't," says the cat

"I won't," says the goose.

"I won't," says the turkey

"I will, then," says the little red hen. So she baked the flour, and made a loaf of bread

"Who will eat this bread?" said the little red hen.

"I will," says the dog.

"I will," says the cat.

"I will," says the goose

"I will," says the turkey

"*I* will," says the little red hen, and she ate the loaf of bread all up

SPELLING

. .

IN the old-time spellin'-school,
that met in some places as often
as once a week, there was one ex-
ercise the spellers frequently went
through in concert. When sides
had been chosen, and the long line
of each of the contending forces
had ranged itself along the school-
room wall, facing its opponent, the
master gave out the word, —

Cisnecristovervanprovant i m t a m t i r e -
liremackfamewelldonesquire. All together the school pronounced the word, and
spelled it as follows, in a resounding
chorus : —

C-i-s, cis; n-e, ne, cisne ; c-r-i-s, cris,
cisnecris; t-o, to, cisnecristo ; v-e-r, ver,
cisnecristover ; v-a-n, van, cisnecristover-
van ; p-r-o, pro, cisnecristovervanpro ;
v-a-n, van, cisnecristovervanprovan ;
t-i-m, tim, cisnecristovervanprovantim ;
t-a-m, tam, cisnecristovervanprovantim-
tam ; t-i-r-e, tire, cisnecristovervanpro-
vantimtamtire ; l-i-r-e, lire, cisnecristo-

vervanprovantimtamtirelire ; m - a - c - k,
mack, cisnecristovervanprovantimtam-
tireliremack ; f-a-m-e, fame, cisnecristover-
vanprovantimtamtireliremackfame ; w-e-
double l, well, cisnecristovervanprovan-
timtamtireliremackfamewell, d - o - n - e,
d o n e, cisnecristovervanprovantimtam-
tireliremackfamewelldone , s - q - u - i - r- e,
squire, cisnecristovervanprovantimtam-
tireliremackfamewelldonesquire !

In some day-schools the word was
also spelled by the scholars in unison,
just after they came in from recess. It
took their attention, and had a quieting
effect on them.

To new scholars the spellin'-master
sometimes put the word " Constantinople." The scholars began, " C-o-n, Con ;
s-t-a-n, stan, Constan ; t-i, ti, Constanti "
— " No," said the teacher at this point;
and the scholar thought he had made a
mistake, and let the word go on to the
next So it went until some one noted
the joke, and saw that the master was
pronouncing the next syllable of the
word.

The word Constantinople was likewise
capable of being put through the following gymnastics —

C-o-n, Con, with a Con , isn t that a

Con ? S-t-a-n, stan, with a stan, isn't
that a stan, and isn't that a Constan?
T-i, ti, with a ti; isn't that a ti, and isn't
that a stanti, and isn't that a Constanti?
N-o, no, with a no; isn't that a no, and
isn't that a ti-no, and isn't that a stan-ti-
no, and isn't that a Con-stan-ti-no? P-l-e,
ple, with a ple; isn't that a ple, and isn't
that a no-ple. and isn't that a ti-no-ple,
and isn't that a stan-ti-no-ple, and isn't
that a Con-stan-ti-no-ple ? and isn't that
a Constantinople ?

" Spell elderblow tea with four letters " was a request sometimes made
fifty years ago

Answer. " L, double o, t."

A third party might comment, " Well,
I c'n spell it with two letters."

First person, " Let's hear you, then."

Answer " I-t, it "

Spell Habakkuk

H and an *a*, and a *b* and an *a*, and a
k and a *k*, and a *u* and a *k*; Habakkuk.

Spell woodchuck

Double u, double u,
Double o, d,
C-h-u-double u,
Double k e ,
    woodchuck

Spell potato

Put one o, put two o, put three o, put four o, put five o, put six o, put seven o, put eight o.

Spell Mississippi.

M-i-double s, i-double s, i-double p-i.

Spell backache.

B-a-c—k-a—c-h-e.

Spell huckleberry pie.

H-u, huckle ; b-u, buckle ; c-u, cuckle ; y ; huckleberry pie.

Spell Tennessee.

One a see, two a see, three a see, four a see, five a see, six a see, seven a see, eight a see, nine a see, Tennessee.

Spell pumpkin-pie.

P double-unkin, p double i ; p double-unkin, punkin-pie.

When a company gathered for an evening, years ago, they sometimes amused themselves by spelling, or learning to spell, the phrase, " Abominable bumble-bee with his tail cut off." Here is the way they spelled it · " *A*, there's your *a* ; b-o, *bo*, there's your *bo* and your *a*-bo ; m-i, *mi*, there's your *mi*, and your *bo*-mi, and your *a*-bo-mi ; n-a, *nā*, there's your *na*, and your *mi*-na, and your *bo*-mi-na, and *a*-bo-mi-na ; b-l-e, ble (pronounced " bell "), there's your *ble*, and your *na*-

ble, and your *mi*-na-ble, and your *bo*-mi-na-ble, and your *a*-bo-mi-na-ble."

Thus they spelled on down to the final syllable, and the matter ended thus : " O double f, *off*, there's your *off*, and your *cut* off, and your *tail* cut off, and your *his* tail cut off, and your *with* his tail cut off, and your *bee* with his tail cut off, and your *ble* bee with his tail cut off, and your *bum*-ble-bee with his tail cut off, and your *ble* bum-ble-bee with his tail cut off, and your *na*-ble bum-ble-bee with his tail cut off, and your *mi*-na-ble bum-ble-bee with his tail cut off, and your *bo*-mi-na-ble bum-ble-bee with his tail cut off, and *there's* your abomi-nable bumblebee with his tail cut off ! "

This spelling was very exciting, tongue-tripping, and laughable, and not many could carry it clear through to the end.

Spelled in the same way was the word, " Ho-no - ri-fi - cabili - ni-tudini - tu - tebus - que."

Also the word " Incomprehensibility."

PROBLEMS

. .

I.

Question. A man wanted to cross a river. He had with him a fox, a goose, and half a bushel of corn. His boat was such that he could only take one of these across at a time. Now, if he left the fox and goose together on either shore, the latter would be eaten. If he left the goose and corn together, the corn would be eaten. How did the man get across and not sacrifice any of his property?

Answer. He carried across the goose first. Then he came back and got the corn. He carried that over, and took the goose back with him. He left the goose, and carried across the fox. Finally he went back and got his goose, and there he was.

II.

Question. A man with an eight-quart pail full of milk and empty five-and-three-quart pails was requested by a friend to sell four quarts. How did he give exact measure with only the help of his three pails.

Answer. He filled the three-quart pail and emptied it into the five. Then he poured out another three-quart pail full and filled the five-quart pail from it. That left one quart in the small pail. Then he emptied the five-quart pail into the big pail and the one-quart into the five-quart pail Next he filled the three-quart pail, and that left four quarts in the large pail.

III.

Question. Three Indians and three white men were travelling together They came to a river, and found a canoe, but the boat would only carry two at a time Now, if more Indians were left on a bank, while a crossing was made, than white men, the latter ran the risk of being treacherously killed. If more white men than Indians were left on a bank while the canoe was crossing, the savages were likely to be foully dealt with. How did the whole party get across, and always have white men and Indians on either bank evenly matched?

Answer. An Indian and a white man

cross first   The Indian is left on the
farther shore, and the white man takes
the canoe back   He gets out, and the
remaining two Indians cross. One of
the Indians brings back the canoe, gets
out, and two white men go over. One
of them gets out, an Indian gets in, and
the two in the canoe go to the other
shore   The white man gets out, and the
two Indians cross.   Now all the Indians
are over, and the single white man on
the farther shore gets in, takes the canoe
over, and brings back a comrade   They
both get out, and one of the Indians
takes the canoe over and brings over the
last of the white men.   The party can
then go on

IV.

Question.

> A goose between two geese,
> And a goose ahead of two geese
> And a goose behind two geese
> How many geese were there ?

Answer. Three.

How many feet have forty sheep, a
shepherd, and a dog ?

Two   Only the shepherd has feet
The sheep have hoofs, and the dog
paws.

Read the following —

　　b e d .

If you do it correctly you will say, "A little dark e in bed."

A man had twenty sick sheep. One died. How many had he left?

Answer Nineteen

Ask this question : —

Which is right, six and five *is* thirteen, or six and five *are* thirteen?

Of course the answer is neither, but the one questioned will puzzle over the use of "is" and "are."

Another puzzler is this —

　　Forty sheep went through a gap ;
　　Forty men went after that ,
　　Six, seven, twice eleven,
　　Three and two, how much is that ?

This makes an extended problem if one attempts to figure from the first line.

What is it has four legs and only one foot ?

A bedstead

　　Mississippi went to town,
　　Mississippi tore her gown ;

All the women in the town
Couldn't mend Mississippi's gown.

What's that ?

Answer. A butterfly.

The spelling of the butterfly in the conundrum is as it appears in the minds of those who do not know the answer. After the answer is given, the proper spelling seems to have been Mrs. Sippi.

OLD SONGS

. .

THE TRAVELLER

I TARRIED all night until the next
    day;
I thought it high time to be jog-
    ging away;
I asked the landlady what was to
    pay.
"Come, kiss me, kind sir and go
    your way."

    Sing bug o' the Dutch,
    Li fal de ding day,
    I' in my pocket but one pennay.

I saw some gentlemen throwing at dice,
I see them throw them once or twice.
As I stood by a-lookin' on,
They took me to be some gentlemon.

    Sing bug o' the Dutch,
    Li fal de ding day,
    I' in my pocket but one pennay.

They had a mind I should throw it
    again,
I had the good fortune for to win.

If they had a-won and I had lost
I should had to pull out an empty puss

> Sing bug o' the Dutch
> Li fal de ding day,
> I' in my pocket but one pennay.

The story here told is fragmentary.
and there were undoubtedly more verses
in the original poem

THE COURTIN'

On Thanksgivin' Day, I've heard them
 say,
I mounted on my dapple gray,
And away I rode to Stanton Green,
To court one farmer's daughter Jane

> Rarefala, rarefala,
> Whack for la for larry for la.

When I arrived unto the hall,
Aloud for my true love I did call ,
And I trust the servant led me in
That I my courtship might begin

> Rarefala, rarefala
> Whack for la for larry for la

" My mammy sent me here to woo,
And I can fancy none but you
If you ll consent and marry me now,
I'll treat you as well as I know how "

Rarefala, rarefala,
Whack for la for larry for la.

" 'Tis I can reap and I can mow,
And I can plough and I can sow,
And away to market to sell my hay,
And that'll bring me twopence a day.'

Rarefala, rarefala,
Whack for la for larry for la.

"Twopence a day will never do,
For I wear silks and satins too,
Besides a coach to take the air " —
Oh, curse the lady, she makes me
stare ! "

Rarefala, rarefala,
Whack for la for larry for la.

" 'Tis silks and satins you shall wear,
Besides a coach to take the air,
And if you won't consent to marry me
to-day,
I'll take my Dobbin and ride away '

Rarefala, rarefala,
Whack for la for larry for la.

" Pray, young Johnny, take me now,
For I can spin and milk your cow,
And away to church on the Sabbath Day,
Johnny and I and the dapple gray "

Rarefala, rarefala,
Whack for la for larry for la.

This song was sung at evening gather-
ings by a single voice   The parts where
the lady spoke were sung in a higher key
than the rest.

THE BALLAD OF LORD LOVELL

As sung in New England in 1830

Lord Lovell he stood at his castle gate,
A-combing his milk-white steed,
When along came Lady Nancy Bell
To wish her fond lover good speed.

" Oh, where are you going, Lord Lovell? "
      she said,
" Oh, where are you going? " said she
" I'm a-going, my Lady Nancy Bell,
Strange countries for to see "

" Oh, when will you be back? ' Lady
      Nancy she said,
" Oh, when will you be back ? " said she.
" In a year or two, or three at the most,
I return to your fair bodee "

He hadn't been gone but a year and a
      day
Strange countries for to see,
When languishing thoughts came into
      his mind,
Lady Nancy Bell he would go see.

He rode and he rode his milk-white
 steed,
Till he came to fair London town,
And there he heard St. Varney's bell,
And the people mourning round.

" Is there any one dead ?" Lord Lovell
 he said ;
" Is there any one dead ? " said he.
"The Lord's daughter is dead," the lady
 replied ;
" And some call her the Lady Nancee."

He ordered the grave to be opened
 forthwith,
And the shroud to be folded down ,
And then he kissed her clay-cold cheeks
Till the tears came trickling down

Lady Nancy she died, as it might be
 to-day,
Lord Lovell he died to-morrow ,
And out of her grave there grew a red
 rose,
And out of Lord Lovell's a brier.

They grew and they grew, till they
 reached the church top,
And so they could grow no higher ;
And there they twined in a true-lover's
 knot,
Which true lovers always admire.

THE HUNTERS OF KENTUCKY

Ye've heard of New Orleans,
Its fame for wealth and beauty,
There's girls of every hue, it seems,
From snowy white to sooty.

We made a little bank of cotton bags,
Not that we were afraid of dying,
But because we choose to rest
Unless the game be flying.

Lord Pachingham, he made his brags,
If he in flight was lucky,
He'd have those girls and cotton bags
In spite of old Kentucky.

Jackson led us down to a cypress
    swamp,
Where the ground was low and mucky.
There stood John Bull in marshalled
    pomp,
Here stood old Kentucky.

Jackson he was wide awake,
And was not scat at trifles;
And well he knew
What aim we take with our Kentucky
    rifles.

They came so near we could see 'em
    wink;

We thought it was time to stop 'em.
Oh, 'twould done you good I think
To see Kentuckians drop 'em !

The above is a fragment of a song
sung in the time of Jackson's political
campaigns

THE SONG OF THE DARBY RAM

As I was goin' to Darby
On a market's day,
I saw the biggest ram, sir,
That was ever fed on hay.
He had four feet to go on,
And also for to stand ,
And every foot he had, sir,
Would cover an acre of land
The wool that grew on his belly
Went dragging to the ground ;
The wool that grew on his back, sir,
Would weigh ten thousand pound

Taralal de do,
Taralal de diddledy,
Taralal de day.

The butcher that butchered this ram, sir,
Was drownded in his blood ,
And he that held the basin
Was carried away in the flood.

The man that owned this ram, sir,
Must needs be very rich,
And the man that made this song, sir,
He died last year with the itch.

> Taralal de do,
> Taralal de diddledy,
> Taralal de day.

THOSE YOUNG MEN

Those young men that trot about the
  town,
You'd think they were worth one thousand pound;
Look in their pockets — not a penny
  you'll find,
False and fickle is a young man's mind.

These young men when they first begin
  to love,
It's nothing but " My Honey " and " My
  Turtle-dove ; "
But once they are married, it's no such
  a thing,
It's trouble, trouble, trouble, and it's
  trouble again

MARCHING TO QUEBEC

The singers marched, went through
several odd manœuvres, and the couples,

as they were chosen, joined hands,
kissed, and went to their seats

We're marching down to old Quebec,
Where the drums are loudly beating,
We shall meet with no attack,
For the British are retreating.
The war's all over,
So we'll turn back,
Nevermore to be parted,
We'll open the ring, and choose a couple
in,
For we trust you're all true-hearted
Now you want a fine companion,
Want to soothe the cares of life;
Now you have a mind to marry,
Choose you one and handsome wife;
Now you're joined in love and friend-
ship,
Love and serve him while he's here,
Kiss, and swear that you'll prove con-
stant
So long as he remains your dear

BILLY BOY

Oh, where have you been, Billy Boy,
Billy Boy?
Oh, where have you been, charming
Billy?

I have been to seek a wife,
She's the joy of my life,
But she's a young thing, and cannot
    leave her ma.

Can she sweep up the house, Billy Boy,
    Billy Boy?
Can she sweep up the house, charming
    Billy?
Yes, she can sweep up the house,
Quick's a cat can catch a mouse;
But she's a young thing, and cannot
    leave her ma.

Can she make mince-pies, Billy Boy,
    Billy Boy?
Can she make mince-pies, charming
    Billy?
Yes, she can make mince-pies
With a very few flies;
But she's a young thing, and cannot
    leave her ma

Second Version

Can she make a pumpkin-pie, Billy Boy,
    Billy Boy?
Can she make a pumpkin-pie, charming
    Billy?
Yes, she can make a pumpkin-pie,
Quick's a cat can wink its eye;

And she's a young thing, and cannot
    leave her mither.

Does she light you up to bed, Billy Boy,
    Billy Boy?
Does she light you up to bed, charming
    Billy?
Yes; she lights me up to bed
With a nightcap on her head,
And she's a young thing, and cannot
    leave her mither

Oh, how old is she, Billy Boy, Billy Boy?
Oh, how old is she, charming Billy?
Twice six, twice seven,
Twice twenty and eleven;
Isn't she the young thing that cannot
    leave her mither!

Neither of these versions is like those
given in the song collections. In old
times, after the usual verses had been
sung, the singers, if they were clever,
would make up new ones.

THE BATTLE OF THE NILE

When an old-time party wished to
amuse itself, it would sometimes be proposed that they all join in singing this
battle-song The words were these:—

Where were you all the while?
Oh, I was at the battle of the Nile,
I was there all the while.

Some one then requests that the company sing the forty-ninth verse of that song. The words are repeated. Other verses are called for, but the joke is that every verse is the same as the first.

OLD STORIES

. .

In the early part of the century, the
people were very fond of telling ghost
stories of an evening about the kitchen
fire, and some people of great general
intelligence were very superstitious. As
an instance, I speak of Squire H——, a
man who was esteemed one of the pillars
of the town. He said of his first wife
that she saw her own apparition. One
winter day she had been washing clothes
in the kitchen. When she had finished
she went to the glass, and combed her
hair. While thus engaged she happened
to look out of the window, and saw herself walking on the snow. The Squire
had gone to the village, but when he
returned he found his wife in tears.
She told him what she had seen, and

said she knew that such an appearance meant she was not to live long. She died within a year.

The Squire's second wife did not believe in witches, and never would accept this story; but the Squire explained her unbelief by stating that she was the first-born in her father's family, and that over such the witches had no power. All authorities agree that to see one's double is a very bad sign   Such affirm that Abraham Lincoln saw his double before he was assassinated, and that he told his friends he knew from that he would not live his term out

The following is an example of an old-time witch story   It involves no less a personage than a clergyman. This clergyman's name was Hooker He was travelling on horseback when, one evening, night overtook him at Springfield, Mass, and he sought an inn   Other travellers were before him; and the landlord informed Rev Mr Hooker that he had only a single vacant room left, and, unfortunately, that room was haunted   The clergyman said he did not mind that, and took the room.

He had retired, and everything was still when twelve o'clock came, and with it the witches. In they flocked through keyholes and cracks, until they filled the room. The visitors brought with them many shining dishes of gold and silver, and prepared for a feast.

When everything was ready they invited the clergyman to partake. Although he knew very well that if he ate with witches he would become one, he accepted the invitation

"But," he said, "it is my habit to ask a blessing before eating," and at once began it.

The witches couldn't stand blessings, and fled helter-skelter, leaving feast and plate in possession of the preacher. Whether he ate the whole feast himself or not is not related. At any rate, Rev. Mr. Hooker secured the gold and silver dishes; and the next morning, while continuing his journey, a crow flapping along overhead shouted to him, "You are Hooker by name, and Hooker by nature, and you've hooked it all"

THE DEVIL AND THE CARD—PLAYERS

In a Connecticut village four men were visiting together one evening At length one of them proposed that they should have a game of cards They were aware of the wickedness of card-playing, and knew very well how scandalous the proposal was. Nevertheless, after a little argument, they agreed to play for a short time. On a stand in the corner of the kitchen was a candle whose flame had eaten nearly down to the socket Said one of the men, "We'll just play till the candle burns out There can't be much harm in that, I'm sure'

"Very good," said the others; "we'll stop when the candle burns out."

They played one game, two games, three games, and still the candle burned. The candle burned, and game followed game until morning came, and the first rays of daylight startled the four players

Then they knew that Satan himself had been their companion through the night Who but the Devil would have kept that candle burning for so many hours for such a purpose?

BEWITCHED CREAM

Daniel Smith was churning. He looked into the churn now and then to see what progress he was making, but the butter was no nearer coming the last time he looked in than it was the first. The suspicion grew on Mr. Smith that there was something uncanny about this fact. The more he thought about it the more certain he became that there was a witch in the cream. To expel this evil spirit he dipped up a little of the cream, and threw it into the fire. Immediately after that the butter came. That same day it was reported that Widow Brown had burned herself. Then Mr. Smith knew it was the Widow Brown who had bewitched his cream

RAISING THE WIND

" My father," said the narrator, "worked for a man in Longmeadow, Mass. The man he worked for was the doctor there. One day the doctor says he guessed he'd send some rye to mill. But the wind didn't blow none so't they could winnow it. In them times they used to have to shake it out-

doors somewhere so't the wind'd blow
the chaff away. There warn't a mite
of wind stirrin' that mornin'; and so the
doctor, he and my father, sot there in
the kitchen a-talkin,' and guessin' they'd
have to let it go till next day. While
they was a-doin' o' this in comes the
doctor's wife, and says the wind was be-
ginnin' to blow up a little. And sure
enough! when they come to go out the
wind was blowin' considerable, and my
father went right to cleanin' up the rye.
There might not be nothin in it, but my
father always thought that woman was a
witch. 'Twarn't nateral the wind should
come up sudden that way, without no
help. That woman she wanted the
flour, and so she just went out and made
the wind blow up the way it did

THE CAT WHICH LOST A CLAW

There was a man by the name of
Jones had a sawmill. He was so driven
with work that he frequently was obliged
to run the saw evenings One night he
was going down to the mill to work; and
his wife said she didn't want him to, but
he went just the same. He got the saw
running, and a log rolled on, when along
came a black cat he'd never seen before.

She purred around very friendly, rubbing up against the man, and trotting along on the log he was sawing. Finally she got to fooling around the saw, and got a claw cut off. Then she ran away up the hill toward the man's house. When the man got through work, and went home, he found his wife had one of her fingers done up. He asked her what the matter was, and she wouldn t tell him. But he kept at her, and after a while she let him see her hand. One finger was cut clean off. Then the man knew his wife was a witch, and that she was that same black cat which got its claw sawed off at the mill.

HOW TO KILL A WITCH

It was a common trick in the olden time of such women as were witches to turn into cats, and go scooting along the top rails of fences. It was useless trying to shoot these witch cats with any ordinary load. Leaden bullets would not touch them. To kill them, the gun had to be loaded with a silver ball. It was needful for the person who went witch-killing to use great care about his ammunition; for they said about the ball, that, —

" If it isn't pure silver
It only maims and doesn t kill her "

CHEATING THE DEVIL

A farmer who had no money wanted
a barn. Indeed, he wanted the barn very
badly The man had just a shed or two
back of his little house, and it did not
seem to him he could get along without
a barn much longer possibly. Now, the
Devil knew very well how the man was
feeling ; and one day he went to the man,
and said he'd build him a barn So
they fixed up a bargain between them
For putting up the barn the Devil was
to have the man's soul when he died ;
but the work must be done before the
first rooster crew in the morning, or the
bargain was off All that night the man
heard the Devil hammering and hammering away up the hill a little ways,
where he was building the barn A
while before daylight the man got up,
and went out the back door to where he
had a slab shed he kept his hens in.
He stopped before the door, and made
an imitation of crowing, and the old
rooster answered him. That knocked
the bargain all to pieces, and the Devil
got well cheated that time The man

got his barn free , but being of the Devil's building I don't suppose it was a very good one, or lasted very long.

THE WILBUR WITCHES

These witches made themselves famous about seventy-five years ago in the hill country of western Massachusetts.

Their pranks were played in a secluded hamlet known as Simpson Hollow, and they particularly afflicted the Wilbur family there The Wilburs were a good, respectable, church-going family; but, by some mysterious dispensation of Providence, they were the ones who had to suffer They would find their Sunday clothes snipped and gashed, for one thing While this witch business was going on, the Wilburs made it a point to look over the clothes they had hung up in the closets and about the rooms each day. One morning, after Mrs Wilbur had made the rounds, she is reported to have said, " Well, I believe there's nothin' this time " The words were no sooner out of her mouth than a skirt dropped down on the floor with a half-yard slash in it.

Granny Bates, who was one of the family, one day missed her gold beads,

and where should they be found but at
the top of the well-sweep

Again the beads were gone They
searched high and low; and finally the
beads were found in a teacup, in the
bottom of a tub of clothes that they had
taken down by the brook to rinse, and
spread on the grass

Another strange thing was that the
family were continually finding odd
articles of one sort and another in the
dye-tub by the kitchen fireplace. This
could not be allowed to go on, and one
of the boys was told to sit on the dye-
tub and stay there, but nothing came
of it.

These stories circulated through the
neighborhood, and occasioned not a
little excitement Even the minister
was a good deal exercised over it. He
led in a number of prayer-meetings at
the house ; but the Devil continued,
nevertheless, in apparent full possession.

Sometimes a watch was set, and this
served to fasten suspicion on Granny
Bates and an old cat owned in the family. When some one went to get meal
to sift, they found this old cat in the bin.
Then they noticed that the old cat had
begun to look very strangely, and there

were those who affirmed that its features bore a very close resemblance to those of Granny Bates.

At last, on one of the nights when a party was trying to drive out the witch- es, this old cat was seen to go through a closed garret window, glass and all, without break- ing a pane. People who saw it said that this was no other than Granny Bates in the form of a black cat. But it was never settled who the witch really was, and some had suspicions of a ser- vant-girl who was working in the fam- ily. It was a good while before the excitement died out; and for a long time after, when anything strange hap- pened in the community, people would say, "Well, that's the Wilbur witches."

A BURN CURED

"Once, when I was a young girl, there was a woman lived in our family who said she could cure burns by talkin' to 'em I used to poke fun to her about it But one day I tipped over a kittle of hot water, and got scalded all along down my arm It hurt so it didn't seem as if I could stan' it, and I begged that woman to do something if she could. She warn't goin' to, because she said I didn't believe she could do anything, and laughed at her But I told her I wouldn't any more, and I'd believe anything if she'd only cure me. So she passed her hands kind o' light back and forth over the burns, and mumbled something, and the pain went away right off I asked her afterwards what it was she said, but she wouldn't tell She said she could only tell it to some man who warn't any of my relation."

DEALING WITH GHOSTS

"If a ghost was to appear to me I wouldn't be afraid of him," said Grandmother Brown; "and if some night some of you children see a ghost, you just tell me. I would know, if a ghost came to me, he either wanted help, or came to

warn me, and I should just ask him
what he wanted Oh, there's no need
of bein' scared of a ghost "

If a ghost appeared to a person, the
proper words in which to address it
were, " What, in the name of God, do
you want?

THE CANNIBAL FROGS

In the early part of the century there
lived a boy in the town of Hadley who
was terribly lazy His name was Ed-
ward Good

One spring evening he was sent on an
errand that took him across a swampy
meadow When he came to this meadow,
the night air was so laden with strange
pipings and croakings that Master Good
became frightened and uneasy in his
mind He hesitated, and listened fearfully to the uncanny noises ; and the result was that the darkness and the weird
voices so scared him that he turned and
ran home

His folks were astonished that so slow
a boy should get home so soon, and
asked him if he had done the errand

He said, " No ; I was goin' to do it,
but I got down in the meadow, and
all the frogs was hollerin', 'Ketch Eddy,

ketch Eddy!   Eat him up, eat him up!'
and I didn't dast to go across."

A SEVERE PUNISHMENT

A stranger came one day to Lonetown
Tavern long ago, and stayed day after
day, and week after week. He did no
work, and seemed to have no business;
he did not even let his name be known.
This was all very puzzling to the towns-
folk, and they were entirely at sea in
their conjectures as to why he was there.

At length the people of the village
sent a delegation to the man to get
some information as to who and what
he was. He would give them no satis-
faction then; but after some talk back
and forth he consented to name a time
when he would answer their various
questions plainly and fully.

On the appointed night the delegation presented itself, and was thus
enlightened   " Gentlemen," said the
stranger, " I am a criminal. I had my
choice at the bar of justice, to be hung
or to spend six months in Lonetown.
I chose to come here, but I wish now
that I had chosen to be hung."

With that the stranger bade the company " Good-evening," and bowed himself out of the room.

THE RIVAL COOKS

In a green valley among the Berkshire hills in days gone by there lived two women in houses less than a quarter of a mile apart, who took great pride in their cooking Each was sure she was the best cook of the two, and their rivalry at length grew so warm that they agreed to have a contest to see which could make the largest pudding. They stewed and brewed and baked with great labor and mystery. The test-day came, and a large company of old and young from all the region about gathered to see and taste the giant puddings The crowd drew up around the festive board, and gazed and commented and ate What the size of the puddings really was is not reported; but we get a hint of their magnitude from the fact that after slice after slice had been cut away from one side of the smallest one, the remainder fell over and killed one of the children at the table

THE WARNING OF THE FROGS

The events chronicled in this narrative occurred in western Massachusetts, in the township of Northampton. Far from any present habitations, on

a marshy meadow, under the eastern
shadow of a rough mountain ridge, is a
half-choked cellar-hole and a few bushy
old apple-trees that show there once
stood a farmhouse.   If inquiry is pur-
sued, it is ascertained that Moses Pomeroy, a hundred years since, owned this
property, and lived there with a numerous family   Among other traditions of
the place, is one having to do with a
certain jug Moses carried to the village
store with considerable regularity to be
filled with rum   One dark night he returned laden with this jug, and came
opposite the marsh, when he was startled
by guttural voices from the pond crying
out, " Pomeroy ! Pomeroy ! Jug o' rum !
jug o' rum ! Got drunk ! got drunk !
Go home ! go home !   These remarks
so worked on the mind of Mr Pomeroy
that he said to himself, " If the very frogs
have got to mocking me, and saying
that I am drunk, I will stop drinking."
Thereupon he swung his jug in air, and
threw it far out into the pond

TIM FELL'S GHOST

Connected with the Ireland Parish
district of the city of Holyoke, Mass,
is a famous ghost story, which runs as

follows: In the old days there lived on
"Back Street" a Mr. Felt. One fall
he sowed a field of rye. The rye came
up well, and in the spring was looking
green and thrifty. He was therefore the
more disturbed at the frequent visits of
Neighbor Hummerston's geese to the
said field

Mr Felt had a quick temper, and this
sort of thing was too much for him He
caught the whole flock one day, killed
them, and then wended his way to Dea-
con Hummerston to inform him what he
had done, and where his geese were to
be found

This and other acts showed his hasty
temper and savage disposition and
brought him into disrepute among his
neighbors He often cruelly beat his
horses and cattle, and there were times
when he served the members of his
family in the same way

He had a son, Timothy by name, a
dull-witted fellow, who was slow of
comprehension, and in his work made
many mistakes. This was a frequent
cause of anger to his father, who on
such occasions would strike Tim to the
earth with whatever implement he happened to have in hand, — a hoe, a rake,

or a pitchfork, perchance. These attacks sometimes drove Tim from home, but, after a few days' absence, necessity would bring him back again. At last, however, he disappeared, and was seen no more; and a little later the Felts moved West.

In building the New Haven and Northampton canal, a great deal of limestone was used. On Mr. Felt's farm was a ledge of this rock, and the company soon had a quarry there The overseer was a rough, ill-tempered fellow, and it was not long before he had trouble with his workmen, and they all left him. That brought work to a standstill, and the overseer was at his wit's end to find some way out of his difficulty.

One night, shortly after the men left, the overseer, on his way home from the corner store. quite late, saw a dark figure standing on the limestone ledge, outlined against the sky The overseer stood still, his frightened gaze riveted on the stranger. Presently he broke the silence by asking, "Who are you? and what is your business?"

The spectre replied, "My name is Timothy Felt, and my bones are under

where I now stand   I was killed by my
father four years ago, and if you will
blast this rock you will find my bones."

This story ran through all the country
round, and created great excitement.
Every day, for some time afterwards,
loads of people, not only from Ireland
Parish, but from towns quite distant,
wended their way thither, inquiring the
way to the "ghost place," and when
night came on people would make a
long detour rather than pass the spot,
and run the risk of meeting Tim's uneasy spirit.   Money was raised to continue the quarrying until Tim's skeleton
should be brought to light, but no bones
were found, and after the overseer had
gotten out what stone he wanted, the
work lagged and was discontinued.

Was this humbug or not?   A certain
old lady used to say —

"Where folks believe in witches, witches
    air ;
But when they don't believe, there are
    none there"

In this case there was wide belief that
Tim was murdered, and that his ghost
did really appear.

THE VILLAGE ROOSTERS AND WILLIAM
SMITH

In one of the old New England towns
there lived in days of yore a youth
named William Smith. William lived
at the lower end of the chief village
street Near the upper end of the same
street lived a young woman with whose
charms William was so smitten that his
calls on her were not only frequent but
protracted

One night when he had made one of
these calls, he sought his home at the
magic hour when, in such towns as had
steeple clocks, the bells tolled twelve.
William had not gone down the street
far when he was startled by the crow
of a rooster But the remarkable thing
was that he clearly detected beneath its
rough notes these words, " The woman
rules here." There was no doubt about
what the rooster said, for it immediately repeated the words, and even more
clearly, "The woman rules here "

While William walked along ponder-
ing this strange statement. he heard the
voice of a second rooster at the next
house below. It said, " The man rules
here. The man rules here."

It was plain to William that he was being let into some of the family secrets of the village. All through the street the roosters greeted him as he passed along. At some of the houses it was the man that was chief, at some the woman. William certainly had food for reflection, but it is not related that he ever made any use of this knowledge which came to him so strangely.

In this connection I may mention that some say if you listen to roosters calling back and forth you can hear this conversation

Rooster at first house. "The women rule here."

Rooster at second house. ' And so they do here.'

Rooster at third house. ' And so they do everywhere '

A grown person, when a rooster crows, will sometimes imitate its call, and work a child's name into the sound. Then he says to the child, " Didn't you hear the rooster calling you ? "

A FORTUNE IN A STICK

There were once three girls who were anxious as to the kind of husbands they should have

At length the eldest said, "You know, sisters, there is a little wood back of the house' Let us all walk through it, and each pick a stick as we go along The one that . picks the handsomest stick will get the handsomest husband "

The others agreed, and off they all three went They had not gone far when the youngest saw a stick that she thought would do well enough for her, and she forthwith picked it. Her sisters walked on and on until they came out of the wood on the other side, but not a stick did they find that was handsome enough to suit them Then all three went home

Not long after the youngest married ; but the eldest two remained single all their lives

The consequence of the general knowledge of this story was, that the old people used sometimes to say to a girl whom they thought over particular in her criticism of the marriageable young men, "You better look out, and not have to go through the woods to pick a stick."

If a woman married a man who was held in low esteem by the community, it was said, "Well, she went through the

wood, and picked a crooked stick after
all "

THE THREE MAIDS WHO WENT TO SEEK THEIR FORTUNES

One time there was three girls went
off to seek their fortunes. They walked
along until they come to a place where
the road split, and went off in three
different directions. The girls sot down
there and talked things over, and then
each one on 'em took one o' the roads

The youngest one she walked along
all day, and it got to be night, and she
stopped at a little house she come to.
There was an old witch woman lived
at that house, but the girl didn't know
nothin' about that. That night she was
moanin' and moanin' because she hadn't
made nothin' that day.

So the next mornin' the old witch
woman told her not to be so downhearted, and she gave her an egg. She
said to the girl that when she got so sor-
rowful she couldn't stan' it any longer,
to break the egg, and it would bring her
good fortin.

The girl took the egg, and travelled
all that mornin', and there never nothin'
happened, and at noon she was so sor-

rowful she broke the egg. It warn't no common egg, and out of it come a little spinnin'-wheel as pretty as could be, and this little wheel would keep spinnin' silk all by itself, without a hand touchin' it.

Along in the afternoon the girl saw a bunch of ladies down by a spring, and she went down to see what they was doin'. They had a handkerchief with blood on it, and they was tryin' to wash it clean, and none of 'em could do it. Then the girl said she would try it, and when she took it, the handkerchief came clean right off

Now, the one that could make that handkerchief clean was to have the king's son for a husband. So they took the girl up to the palace, and she was married to the king's son. But this prince was under an enchantment for seven years. In the daytime he was in the form of a bull, and it was only in the night that he was a man. For seven years the girl had to lead her husband every mornin' away to the stable. At sunset he would come back again a man. But when the seven years was up, then they were all right

Those other two girls that took the

other two roads went along, I don't
know how far; but they never come to
nothin', and they never got married at
all.

"SOMETIME"

One spring day Mr. and Mrs. Robin
were talking over plans for nest-build-
ing An old apple-tree near a farmhouse had been their home for many
years past.

" Better settle down in the same old
tree," said Mr. Robin. · There isn't another in the neighborhood has crotches
to equal it."

"I know it," replied Mrs. Robin;
"but the man who lives in the farmhouse says he's going to build a barn
right here, and our tree would have to
come down."

"When did he say he was going to
build it ? " asked Mr. Robin

"He didn't say just when," Mrs.
Robin answered ; "he said ' *sometime.*' "

"Oh, well," remarked Mr Robin, "we
can have our nest here all right then ; "
and they began to build it in a crotch of
the old apple-tree that very day.

MRS. STOWE'S ORANGES

It is said that the year after Harriet Beecher Stowe's " Uncle Tom's Cabin " came out, all the oranges that grew in her Florida grove were black skinned. There was a good deal of joking in consequence, and the fruit was spoken of as " abolition oranges "

STUMPING THE DEVIL

There was a place where my mother was livin' once, where the whoopin'-cough took and run through the family. It ketched 'em all, little and big, except the hired man, who might have been eighteen or twenty years old.

One day my mother says to him, "Ain't you goin' to have the whoopin'-cough, John ? "

And he says, " No ; I'll stump the Devil to give it to me."

The next thing they knew, John had the whooping-cough, and had it bad. It made him so cross-eyed that you might think he was lookin' all around the lots when he was lookin' straight at you. He never could talk straight after it, and he couldn't walk straight. He kind o' petered out every way. He was a smart, good-lookin' fellow before he had the whoopin'-cough, but that spoilt him. He said he never'd stump the Devil again. I know when he was an old man, eighty years old or so, he used to tell about it and say, " I think I stumped the Devil a little too hard that time "

THE STEERS THAT WOULDN'T DRAW

My mother's father was down in the woods one time, and he'd got his sled loaded up with a little jag o' logs. When he come to start, the steers wouldn't budge. 'Twa'n't much of a load, and he knew the steers could draw it well as not. Now, there was an old woman that lived in the neighborhood that he'd always thought was kind of a witch, and when the steers acted that way he was pretty sure that old woman had bewitched 'em. So he said to himself that he'd cut a stick, and he'd make those steers draw that load or he'd kill 'em. Well, you know if you drawed blood on a thing that was bewitched, you drawed blood on the witch too and if you killed a thing that was bewitched, you killed the witch.

My mother's father was just goin' to give those steers a weltin' when there

come a sort of a low laugh from down
somewhere in the woods. It was that
old witch woman, though she wa'n't
really anywhere around there. As soon
as the steers heard that ar laugh, they
started right along.

THE POWER OF FANCY

It is told of a party of students at
Harvard long ago, that they one day fell
into a dispute as to whether a man could
be made sick through his imagination.
Some said he could, and others said
he couldn't. To settle the dispute they
agreed to try the experiment on a driver
who was well known to all of them, and
who made many trips each week between Cambridge and Boston. The
students stationed themselves along the
road at intervals, so that they might
meet the driver on one of these trips.

Student number one presently sighted
the man and said, " How do you do to-
day ? "

" Oh, I'm as well as usual," says the
driver.

" You don't look as well," responded
the student, and passed on.

Student number two greeted the driver
in the same way, and this conversation

was in substance repeated with every
student in the plot The result was
that this stout, hearty man was over-
powered by the weight of evidence. It
broke him down, and ruined his health.

A GHOST STORY

This should be told in as sepulchral
tones as the teller is capable of, and a
doleful groan should be put in occasionally

There was an old woman, all skin and
    bones,
Who went to church to pray.
First she went half-way up the aisle,
And prayed a little while,
Then she went down to the door,
And prayed a little more ;
And there she saw a ghost upon the
    floor
And she asked the ghost, " Will I look
    like that when I am dead ? "
And the ghost said, " YES ! "

The final word of the story should be
a sudden shout. Some say " Boo ! " instead of " Yes," and others just screech
without definite words.

I give below a more elaborate version

of the same tale. "Do you want to
hear a story?" says the teller. "Well"—

There was an old woman, all skin and
      bones,
Who thought she'd go to church one
      day,
And hear the parson preach and pray.
When she got to the churchyard stile
She thought she'd rest a little while;
And when she got to the church door
She thought she'd rest a little more.
So she looked up, and she looked down,
And she saw a corpse upon the ground.
Then the woman to the parson said,
" Shall I look so when I am dead?"
And the parson to the woman said,
" You will look so when you are dead."
Then the woman to the parson said,
      "OH–H !"

Milton Keynes UK
Ingram Content Group UK Ltd.
UKHW022241270723
425924UK00004B/108